marie claire

easy

Published by Murdoch Books Pty Limited.
www.murdochbooks.com.au

Murdoch Books Australia
Pier 8/9, 23 Hickson Rd
Millers Point NSW 2000
Phone: +61 (0)2 8220 2000
Fax: +61 (0)2 8220 2558

Murdoch Books UK Limited
Erico House, 6th Floor North
93–99 Upper Richmond Road
Putney, London SW15 2TG
Phone: +44 (0)20 8785 5995
Fax: +44 (0)20 8785 5985

Author and Stylist: Michele Cranston
Photographer: Petrina Tinslay
Design manager: Vivien Valk
Concept: Lauren Camilleri
Designer: Jacqueline Richards
Editor: Jacqueline Blanchard
Food preparation: Ross Dobson and Jo Glynn
Production: Monika Paratore

Chief executive: Juliet Rogers
Publisher: Kay Scarlett

National Library of Australia Cataloguing-in-Publication Data
Cranston, Michele. Marie Claire easy. Includes index.
ISBN 1 74045 750 1 / 978 1 74045 750 7
1. Cookery. I. Title. II. Title: Marie Claire (North Sydney, N.S.W.). 641.5

Printed by 1010 Printing International Ltd. Printed in China. First printed 2006.

Text © Michele Cranston 2006. Photography © Petrina Tinslay 2006.
Design © Murdoch Books 2006.
marie claire © STE MARIE CLAIRE ALBUM – S.A.

Important: Those who might be at risk from the effects of salmonella poisoning (the elderly, pregnant women, young children and those suffering from immune deficiency diseases) should consult their doctor with any concerns about eating raw eggs.

Conversion guide: You may find cooking times vary depending on the oven you are using. For fan-forced ovens, as a general rule, set the oven temperature to 20°C (35°F) lower than indicated in the recipe. We have used 20 ml (4 teaspoon) tablespoon measures. If you are using a 15 ml (3 teaspoon) tablespoon, for most recipes the difference will not be noticeable. However, for recipes using baking powder, gelatine, bicarbonate of soda (baking soda) or small amounts of flour and cornflour, add an extra teaspoon for each tablespoon specified.

marie claire
easy

michele cranston
photography by petrina tinslay

MURDOCH BOOKS

contents

Welcome to *marie claire easy*, a selection of our favourite recipes that are simple and light, fruity and sublime, quickly grilled and lightly tossed with a twist of lemon and lime. A hearty book with lots of yummy ideas that we hope will inspire you, with everything from coconut prawns and chilli corn cakes to duck soup and seared snapper, tropical fruit salad and mango jellies.

I've had a lot of fun revisiting old favourites and I hope that you have as much fun cooking and eating from our selection.

michele cranston

ingredient note **papaya and mango**

Tropical fruits are one of the great delights of summer. After months of making do with apples, pears and oranges there is suddenly an explosion on supermarket shelves of all things sweet, colourful and exotically perfumed. Think mangoes, melons, lychees, pineapples, mangosteens and red papayas.

Chilled red papaya is a taste of summer and the tropics. One mouthful can transport you to days of clear skies and endless blue horizons. I love this fruit served simply with a squeeze of lime for breakfast or sliced into a tropical fruit salad. This is a fruit that loves a bit of pepper, so toss it into a bowl with rocket (arugula), prosciutto, basil leaves and a sweet balsamic vinaigrette or simply add it to a chicken salad.

The first mango of the season is always a taste of good things to come. Richly sweet with a tangy bite, the mango needs only to be chilled and cut to make the perfect finish to a summertime dinner. You can also purée the flesh and serve it with ice cream or fold it through creamy yoghurt to have with crisp almond bread. To enhance that summertime taste, finely dice the flesh and add it to a chilli salsa for a wonderful accompaniment to grilled fish or chicken.

ingredient note   # lemon

I'm often asked to name ingredients that I can't do without, and my answer is always the same — fresh herbs and lemon. No matter what time of year, you'll always find lemons in my kitchen. To me, they bring a freshness and vitality of flavour to any recipe they are used in.

Lemon zest contains the oils that perfume the lemon, while the juice contains the flavour. By using a combination of both you heighten the citrus taste. Imagine seafood without lemon, or a dessert selection without the classic lemon tart. Smoked salmon loves a dollop of lemon mayonnaise and my favourite crepe comes with just a splash of lemon juice and a sprinkle of sugar. It's also wonderful added to a simple pasta salad of fresh herbs and parmesan cheese or a bowl of steamed couscous flavoured with coriander and roast almonds. Lemon also makes a perfect base for chicken and seafood marinades, and there are some vegetables that are lost without its acidic tang — think asparagus, broccoli, spinach and zucchini (courgette). The grated zest of the lemon brings a citrus bite to cakes and icing and helps to cut the sweetness of many fruit desserts, so always keep lemons at the ready.

pumpkin

I know it's an everyday vegetable but roast pumpkin (winter squash) is one of my all-time favourites. When looking for pumpkin for roasting I favour those with a firm flesh that is strongly coloured, like the jap (kent). You don't have to do much to this vegetable to make it taste great. Some oil and seasoning will do the trick, but you can also flavour roast pumpkin with soy and ginger or add some cumin and garlic to the roasting oil.

Baked pumpkin is ideal for adding to salads that have a bit of bite. Slightly bitter leaves — think rocket (arugula), radicchio and witlof (chicory/Belgian endive) — will be helped with the addition of pumpkin and the crunch of some nuts. It goes wonderfully with hazelnuts, sunflower seeds, sesame seeds, pecan nuts and cashews. When it comes to the winter months, nothing beats a comforting bowl of warmly spiced pumpkin soup. And let's not forget its close relationship to the zucchini (courgette) and small squashes, which provide a dash of colour and shape to the vegetable repertoire. Smothered with butter, a squeeze of lemon juice and a sprinkle of seasoning they make a wonderful side dish.

ingredient note orange and mandarin

Oranges and mandarins have become such common fruits that it is difficult to appreciate just how exotic they once were. Their flavour has taken hold in European cuisines — as a dried peel, orange is evident in most traditional fruitcakes while the sugared zest is often used to adorn desserts.

Citrus flavours can be used in a variety of ways. They can reduce the richness of meats such as ham, roast pork and spiced duck, or they can be enjoyed purely for themselves. A popular favourite is a bowl piled with segments of orange, grapefruit, mandarin and lime, drizzled with honey and a dollop of creamy yoghurt. Or make a simple savoury salad of watercress, grated beetroot and sliced orange as a side dish.

Citrus flavours also work well with spices like cinnamon, star anise, cloves and cardamom. Add grated orange zest to sweetened mascarpone cheese or enjoy the simple pleasures of an orange or grapefruit sorbet. When a dessert calls for the use of orange it is often nice to add a bit of a twist by using mandarin instead. The mandarin has a slightly more perfumed flavour and will surprise and delight the taste buds.

walnut and soda bread stuffed mushrooms pumpkin muffins

with marmalade corn bread walnut cornbread with bacon

honeyed nuts scrambled egg tartlets potato latkes with

smoked salmon coconut prawns ceviche with coconut dressing

duck and marmalade turnovers salmon in pastry pickled

salmon patate pizza prawn toasts citrus scallop wontons

seared salmon on brioche with saffron mayonnaise squid

stuffed with lemon risotto prawn balls steamed

01   starters and sides

prawn wontons ma hor on pineapple pistachio and orange

crackers goat's cheese tartlets chicken and mushroom

wontons chilli corn cakes sweet pork wontons corn and

prawn pancakes whiting and pumpkin tempura artichoke

tartlets fish cakes prawn sandwich tiny brioche with garlic

walnut and soda bread

makes 1 loaf

450 g (1 lb/3²/₃ cups) plain
(all-purpose) flour
1 heaped teaspoon bicarbonate of
soda (baking soda)
1 heaped teaspoon cream of tartar
1 tablespoon sugar
1 teaspoon sea salt
500 ml (17 fl oz/2 cups) buttermilk
4 tablespoons finely chopped walnuts
40 g (1¹/₂ oz) butter
extra butter, softened, to serve

Preheat the oven to 200°C (400°F/ Gas 6). Put the plain flour, bicarbonate of soda, cream of tartar, sugar and sea salt into a large bowl. Make a well in the centre and gradually add the buttermilk, combining to form a soft dough. Add the walnuts and slowly fold through the dough.

Melt the butter and brush the insides of a 21 x 10 cm (8¹/₄ x 4 in) loaf (bar) tin with the melted butter. Put the dough into the greased tin and pour over any remaining butter.

Bake for 30 minutes, then reduce the oven temperature to 150°C (300°F/Gas 2) and bake for a further 30 minutes, or until a skewer inserted into the centre comes out clean. Turn out the bread onto a wire rack to cool. Serve warm or toasted with butter, apricot jam, honey or ricotta cheese.

stuffed mushrooms   makes 18

60 g (2¹/₄ oz/¹/₄ cup) ricotta cheese
¹/₂ teaspoon finely chopped marjoram
¹/₄ teaspoon finely chopped rosemary
2 slices prosciutto, finely sliced
2 teaspoons virgin olive oil
18 button mushrooms

Preheat the oven to 180°C (350°F/ Gas 4). In a small bowl, combine the ricotta, herbs, prosciutto and oil. Season well with salt and freshly ground black pepper. Remove the stems from the mushrooms and trim their rounded tops with a sharp knife to give them a flat base when put upside down. Spoon the ricotta filling into the centre of the mushrooms and put them on a baking tray. Lightly season with salt and pepper and bake for 12–15 minutes.

pumpkin muffins
with marmalade

makes 36

300 g (10¹/2 oz) pumpkin (winter
   squash), peeled and cut into chunks
155 g (5¹/2 oz/1¹/4 cups) self-raising
   flour
¹/2 teaspoon grated nutmeg
115 g (4 oz/¹/2 cup) caster (superfine)
   sugar
1 large egg
2 tablespoons plain yoghurt
35 g (1¹/4 oz) butter, melted
50 g (1³/4 oz/¹/3 cup) pine nuts, toasted
extra butter, softened, to serve
bitter orange marmalade, to serve

Put the pumpkin in a saucepan of water and boil until tender. Drain and mash the pumpkin.

Preheat the oven to 180°C (350°F/ Gas 4). Sift the flour, nutmeg and a pinch of salt into a large bowl, stir in the sugar and make a well in the centre of the mixture. In a separate bowl, beat together the egg, yoghurt, mashed pumpkin and melted butter. Pour into the well of the flour mixture. Stir until just combined. Gently stir through the pine nuts and spoon into 36 greased mini muffin tins (lined with paper cases if desired). Bake for 10–12 minutes, then cool on a wire rack. Slice in half, butter and spread with bitter orange marmalade.

corn bread

makes 1 loaf

125 ml (4 fl oz/1/2 cup) milk
90 g (31/4 oz) butter
250 g (9 oz/2 cups) plain (all-purpose)
  flour
2 teaspoons baking powder
2 teaspoons bicarbonate of soda
  (baking soda)
250 g (9 oz/12/3 cups) fine polenta
1 teaspoon sea salt
2 eggs
125 ml (4 fl oz/1/2 cup) buttermilk
1 handful of coriander (cilantro) leaves,
  roughly chopped
2 red chillies, seeded and finely
  chopped

Preheat the oven to 180°C (350°F/ Gas 4). Put the milk into a saucepan with the butter. Heat over low heat until the butter has melted, then remove from the heat.

Sift the flour, baking powder and bicarbonate of soda into a bowl. Add the fine polenta and sea salt and make a well in the centre.

In a separate bowl, whisk together the eggs, buttermilk, coriander and chillies. Fold the buttermilk mixture through the dry ingredients, then fold through the warm milk mixture. Pour the batter into a greased 24 cm (91/2 in) spring-form cake tin and mark the top into wedges. Bake for 25 minutes, or until the cornbread is golden brown and a skewer inserted into the centre comes out clean. Serve warm with crispy bacon and roasted tomatoes.

walnut cornbread
with bacon
makes 48

1 tablespoon walnut oil
250 ml (9 fl oz/1 cup) milk
90 g (3¼ oz) unsalted butter
5 slices bacon, finely sliced
250 g (9 oz/1⅔ cups) polenta
310 g (11 oz/2½ cups) plain
  (all-purpose) flour
2 teaspoons baking powder
1 teaspoon bicarbonate of soda
  (baking soda)
3 eggs
100 g (3½ oz/⅓ cup) plain yoghurt
3 spring onions (scallions), finely sliced
85 g (3 oz/⅔ cup) coarsely chopped
  walnuts
extra butter, to serve

Preheat the oven to 180°C (350°F/
Gas 4). Lightly grease two 12-hole
mini muffin tins with walnut oil. Warm
the milk and butter in a small
saucepan. When the butter has
melted, remove from the heat.

Put the bacon in a frying pan and
cook until it has browned but is not
crisp. Remove from the heat.

Meanwhile, sift the dry ingredients and
½ teaspoon of salt into a mixing bowl
and make a well in the centre. Whisk
the eggs with the yoghurt and warm
milk and fold into the dry ingredients
until just blended. Add the spring
onions, walnuts and bacon and lightly
fold through the batter.

Spoon half the mixture into the
greased tins (lined with paper cases if
desired) and bake for 15–20 minutes,
or until firm and golden. Repeat with
the remaining mixture. Serve warm,
spread with butter.

honeyed nuts   serves 4

2 tablespoons honey
1 teaspoon butter
80 g (2³/4 oz/¹/2 cup) almonds
80 g (2³/4 oz/¹/2 cup) pine nuts
60 g (2¹/4 oz/¹/2 cup) sunflower seeds
80 g (2³/4 oz/¹/2 cup) sesame seeds
squeeze of lemon juice
plain yoghurt, to serve

In a small saucepan, warm the honey and butter. Add the nuts and seeds, and stir over low heat until well coated. Remove from the heat and squeeze over a little lemon juice. Serve with yoghurt.

scrambled egg tartlets

makes 24

2 slices prosciutto, each sliced into
  12 pieces
4 eggs
185 ml (6 fl oz/³/₄ cup) cream
  (whipping)
30 g (1 oz) butter
24 pre-baked mini tart shortcrust
  pastry shells (basics)

Preheat the oven to 180°C (350°F/ Gas 4). Put the prosciutto on a baking tray lined with baking paper and grill (broil) or bake until crisp. Remove and drain on paper towel.

Put the eggs and cream in a bowl and lightly whisk together. Season well with salt and pepper. Put half the butter in a non-stick frying pan over medium heat and add half the egg mixture. Slowly fold together. When just set, remove from the heat. Spoon the cooked mixture into half of the pre-baked tart shells and top each tart with a piece of prosciutto. Grease the pan with the remaining butter and repeat the process with the rest of the egg mixture. Serve immediately.

potato latkes
with smoked salmon   makes 45

45 g (1 1/2 oz) butter
2 leeks, white part only, finely chopped
2 tablespoons thyme leaves
390 g (13 3/4 oz/2 1/2 cups) peeled and
    grated potato
2 eggs, lightly beaten
40g (1 1/2 oz/1/3 cup) plain (all-purpose)
    flour
vegetable oil, for cooking
150 g (5 1/2 oz) smoked salmon

Heat the butter in a small saucepan, add the leeks and thyme and cook over low heat for 15–20 minutes, stirring occasionally, until the leeks are soft and slightly caramelized. Set aside to cool.

Mix together the grated potato, eggs and flour and season well with salt and freshly ground black pepper. Put the mixture into a sieve over a bowl and press down to remove any excess moisture.

Add enough vegetable oil to a frying pan to cover the base by 5 mm (1/4 in). Heat the oil over medium heat and add heaped teaspoons of the potato mixture. Flatten a little and cook each side for 4–5 minutes or until golden, and drain on paper towel. Repeat until all the mixture has been cooked.

To assemble, cut the salmon into 45 x 5 mm (1/4 in) lengths. Put a slice of salmon on each latke and top with a small amount of leek.

coconut prawns   makes 20

4 egg whites
125 g (4 1/2 oz/1 cup) plain (all-purpose)
  flour
100 g (3 1/2 oz/1 cup) desiccated
  coconut
170 ml (5 1/2 fl oz/2/3 cup) oil
20 raw prawns (shrimp), peeled and
  deveined
sweet chilli and ginger sauce, to serve
lime wedges, to serve

Whisk the egg whites until they are light and fluffy. Put the flour and coconut onto two separate plates. Heat a deep pan or wok and add the oil. While the oil is heating, toss one of the prawns in the flour, dip it into the egg white, and then roll it in the coconut. Set it aside. Repeat the process with the remaining prawns.

Once the oil has reached frying point (if you drop a coconut shred into the oil it will sizzle), carefully lower the prawns into the oil in batches of five. When the coconut has turned light brown on one side, turn the prawns over and cook until they are crisply golden on both sides. Remove the prawns and drain them on paper towel.

Serve with sweet chilli and ginger sauce and a squeeze of fresh lime.

ceviche with coconut dressing

makes 40

500 g (1 lb 2 oz) firm white-fleshed fish,
  skin removed and boned
3 limes, juiced
100 ml (3½ fl oz) coconut cream
1 teaspoon grated fresh ginger
½ teaspoon ground turmeric
1 teaspoon sugar
1 tablespoon finely chopped coriander
  (cilantro) root
2 spring onions (scallions), finely sliced
  on the diagonal

Slice the fish into bite-sized pieces and put in a glass or ceramic dish. Cover with lime juice and refrigerate for 2 hours. Put the coconut cream, ginger, turmeric, sugar, coriander root and ½ teaspoon of salt in a bowl and stir to combine. Drain the fish and add to the coconut dressing. Sprinkle with the spring onion and serve.

duck and marmalade turnovers

makes 30

20 g (³/₄ oz) butter
155 g (5¹/₂ oz/1 cup) finely chopped onions
1 garlic clove, crushed
50 g (1³/₄ oz) pancetta, finely diced
1 teaspoon thyme leaves
125 ml (4 fl oz/¹/₂ cup) red wine
240 g (8³/₄ oz) whole duck breast fillet, finely diced
2 tablespoons bitter orange marmalade
25 g (1 oz/¹/₄ cup) almond meal
30 shortcrust pastry rounds, 8 cm (3 in) in diameter (basics)
1 egg, beaten

Heat the butter in a small frying pan over medium heat. Add the onion and garlic and cook for 5–7 minutes, or until the onion is transparent. Add the pancetta and thyme and cook for a further 5 minutes before adding the red wine and diced duck breast. Reduce the heat to low and simmer, covered, for 20 minutes, or until the liquid has been absorbed. Remove the cover and return the heat to medium. Add the marmalade and almond meal, stir and cook for 2 minutes, or until the mixture has thickened. Remove from the heat and season with salt and black pepper. Set aside to cool.

Preheat the oven to 180°C (350°F/ Gas 4). Brush the edges of the pastry rounds with beaten egg. Put a heaped teaspoon of the filling in the centre of each pastry round and fold in half. Seal the edges with a fork and put the turnovers on a baking tray lined with baking paper. Brush with more beaten egg and bake for 20 minutes or until golden brown.

salmon in pastry

300 g (10½ oz) whole salmon fillet,
  skin removed and boned
2 teaspoons sumac
1 teaspoon grated fresh ginger
100 g (3½ oz) unsalted butter, cut into
  cubes and softened
1 tablespoon glacé ginger, finely
  chopped
1 tablespoon currants
1 makrut (kaffir lime) leaf, finely sliced
2 sheets ready-made puff pastry,
  thawed
2 tablespoons milk

Preheat the oven to 200°C (400°F/ Gas 4). Cut the salmon lengthways into four 2 cm (¾ in) wide strips. Put the sumac, ginger, softened butter, glacé ginger, currants and makrut leaf in a bowl and mix until soft and well combined.

Slice the pastry sheets in half and lie a piece of salmon along the centre of each one. Top each with a quarter of the flavoured butter and fold the pastry around the salmon, pressing the edges together at the top to form a seal. Put the salmon parcels on a baking tray lined with baking paper, ensure that the pastry is well sealed, and brush with a little milk. Bake for 20–25 minutes, or until golden brown. Remove and allow to cool until just warm. Slice into 2.5 cm (1 in) portions and serve.

pickled salmon

2 tablespoons sweet Japanese pickled
ginger juice
2 teaspoons pickled ginger, finely
sliced
1 tablespoon grated fresh ginger
1 teaspoon light soy sauce
1 teaspoon fish sauce
2 tablespoons lime juice
100 g (3³/4 oz) whole salmon fillet,
boned and skin removed
1 tablespoon finely chopped mint
leaves
30 witlof (chicory/Belgian endive)
leaves, washed and drained
2 teaspoons toasted sesame seeds

In a small bowl, combine the ginger juice, pickled ginger, fresh ginger, soy sauce, fish sauce and lime juice.

Slice the salmon in half lengthways and then slice each half thinly. Put the salmon in the ginger dressing and allow to marinate for 5–10 minutes. Add the mint leaves and toss to combine. Put a tablespoon of the mixture into each of the witlof leaves. Sprinkle with the toasted sesame seeds and serve immediately.

patate pizza

4 potatoes, peeled and finely sliced
2 ready-made medium pizza bases
extra virgin olive oil
1 tablespoon finely chopped rosemary
sea salt, to sprinkle

Preheat the oven to 200°C (400°F/ Gas 6). Arrange the potato slices on the pizza bases. Drizzle liberally with extra virgin olive oil and scatter with the rosemary. Sprinkle with sea salt and bake for 20 minutes. Remove from the oven and drizzle with a little olive oil. This simple pizza is wonderful partnered with hearty winter soups or served as a pre-dinner snack.

prawn toasts

makes 32

250 g (9 oz) raw prawn (shrimp) meat
1 garlic clove, crushed
2 tablespoons chopped spring onions
   (scallions)
1 teaspoon grated fresh ginger
1 teaspoon sugar
1 teaspoon sesame oil
3 teaspoons cornflour (cornstarch)
2 teaspoons finely chopped coriander
   (cilantro) leaves
1 teaspoon grated lemon zest
8 slices white bread, crusts removed
2 tablespoons sesame seeds,
   to sprinkle
peanut oil, for frying

Put the prawn meat, garlic, shallots, ginger, sugar, sesame oil, cornflour, coriander, lemon zest and 1 teaspoon of salt in a food processor and process in short bursts until the mixture is smooth and well mixed.

Cut each slice of bread into quarters, spread the prawn mixture thickly on each square and sprinkle with the sesame seeds.

Put oil in a frying pan to a depth of 1 cm (1/2 in). Heat the oil over moderate heat and cook the bread, prawn side down, until golden. Turn and quickly cook the other side. Serve hot.

citrus scallop wontons

300 g (10¹/₂ oz) white scallop meat
¹/₂ teaspoon grated orange zest
3 tablespoons finely chopped
  coriander (cilantro) leaves
3 tablespoons finely sliced spring
  onions (scallions)
¹/₄ teaspoon sesame oil
1 large red chilli, seeded and
  finely chopped
1 teaspoon fish sauce
1 makrut (kaffir lime) leaf, finely sliced
¹/₄ teaspoon finely grated fresh ginger
2 tablespoons plain (all-purpose) flour
30 square wonton wrappers
peanut oil, for deep-frying
lime wedges, to serve

Dice the scallop meat and put it into a bowl with the orange zest, coriander, spring onions, sesame oil, chilli, fish sauce, makrut lime and ginger. Stir to combine, then sprinkle over the plain flour and stir again.

Put 1 square wonton wrapper on a clean surface and moisten the edges with a little water. Place 1 teaspoon of the filling in the centre, then bring the four corners together, sealing the sides. Repeat with the remaining mixture. Put the wontons on a tray lined with baking paper. To cook, deep-fry in the peanut oil and serve with fresh lime wedges.

seared salmon on brioche with saffron mayonnaise

makes 20

5 x 2 cm (³/₄ in) slices of brioche loaf,
  crusts removed
20 saffron threads
2 egg yolks
2 teaspoons lemon juice
200 ml (7 fl oz) vegetable oil
200 g (7 oz) salmon fillet
2 teaspoons olive oil, for frying
20 sprigs chervil, to serve

Cut each slice of brioche into four squares. Put the saffron in a small saucepan with 60 ml (2 fl oz/¹/₄ cup) of water. Put over medium heat and reduce until only a tablespoon of liquid remains. Remove from the heat and allow to cool. Put the egg yolks and lemon juice in a blender and season with salt and pepper. Blend, and with the motor still running, slowly drizzle in the oil until a thick mayonnaise forms. Pour into a bowl and fold through the saffron water and threads. Set aside. Season the salmon with salt and pepper. Heat the oil in a frying pan over high heat and sear the salmon on both sides, turning once. Reduce the heat and cook for a further 5 minutes. Cool and break the fish up into flakes. Lightly toast the brioche squares. Top with a little of the mayonnaise, some salmon and a sprig of chervil.

squid stuffed with lemon risotto

makes 24 slices

750 ml (26 fl oz/3 cups) fish or
  vegetable stock (basics)
30 g (1 oz) butter
155 g (5^1/2 oz/1 cup) finely diced onion
1 garlic clove, crushed
1 teaspoon thyme leaves
220 g (7^3/4 oz/1 cup) arborio (risotto)
  rice
3 teaspoons finely chopped lemon zest
2 tablespoons lemon juice
15 g (^{1}/2 oz/^{1}/2 cup) roughly chopped
  flat-leaf (Italian) parsley
6 medium squid, each approximately
  15 cm (6 in) long

Preheat the oven to 180°C (350°F/ Gas 4). Heat the stock in a saucepan and keep at a low simmer. Melt the butter in a separate saucepan over moderate heat and cook the onion, garlic and thyme, stirring occasionally, for 5–7 minutes, or until the onion is transparent. Add the rice and zest and stir well until coated. Add 125 ml (4 fl oz/^{1}/2 cup) of hot stock and stir constantly over medium heat until all the liquid has been absorbed. Continue adding more liquid, half a cup at a time, until all the liquid has been absorbed and the rice is creamy and tender. Remove from the heat and add the lemon juice, parsley, salt and freshly ground black pepper.

Clean the squid, removing the tentacles from the body. Stuff the body with the risotto and put in a baking dish with 125 ml (4 fl oz/ ^{1}/2 cup) of water or stock. Cover with foil and bake for 30 minutes. Remove and allow to cool a little before slicing at 2 cm (^{3}/4 in) intervals.

prawn balls

45 g (1$^1/2$ oz/$^1/4$ cup) rice flour
24 large raw prawns (shrimp), shelled
  and deveined
2$^1/2$ teaspoons mirin
1 egg white, lightly beaten
20 g ($^3/4$ oz/$^1/3$ cup) finely sliced spring
  onions (scallions)
100 g (3$^1/2$ oz) somen noodles, broken
  into small pieces
100 ml (3$^1/2$ fl oz) peanut oil

dipping sauce
2 tablespoons lime juice
2 tablespoons mirin
4 tablespoons soy sauce

Sift the flour and $^1/4$ teaspoon of salt into a bowl. Make a well in the centre and gradually add 2 tablespoons of water, whisking to make a smooth paste. Set aside.

Mince or finely chop the prawn meat. Put in a bowl and stir through the mirin, egg white, spring onions and the flour paste. Season with salt and freshly ground black pepper and mix well to combine.

Spread the broken noodles on a sheet of baking paper. Roll $^1/2$-tablespoon amounts of the prawn mix into balls and then roll them in the broken noodles. Set aside.

To make the sauce, combine the lime juice, mirin and soy.

Heat the oil in a wok or deep frying pan over medium heat and cook the prawn balls until golden, turning if necessary. Drain on paper towel and serve with the dipping sauce.

steamed prawn wontons makes 24

2 egg whites
300 g (10 1/2 oz) minced (ground) prawn
  (shrimp) meat
1/2 teaspoon sea salt
1/4 teaspoon Chinese five-spice
30 g (1 oz/1/2 cup) finely sliced spring
  onions (scallions)
1 teaspoon finely grated fresh ginger
24 square wonton wrappers
lemon dipping sauce (basics), to serve

Lightly whisk the egg whites in a large bowl. Add the minced prawn meat, sea salt, five-spice, spring onions and ginger. Stir to combine.

Put 1 square wonton wrapper onto a clean surface and moisten the edges with a little water. Put 1 heaped teaspoon of the filling mixture into the centre of the wrapper and then bring the four corners together, sealing the sides. Set aside and repeat with the remaining mixture.

Put the wontons into a bamboo steamer basket lined with oiled baking paper. Set the basket over a large saucepan of boiling water and steam for 10–12 minutes. Serve with a lemon dipping sauce.

ma hor on pineapple   makes 20

2 garlic cloves, roughly chopped
2 tablespoons roughly chopped
   coriander (cilantro) root
1/2 teaspoon green peppercorns
1 teaspoon grated fresh ginger
2 spring onions (scallions), chopped
2 tablespoons peanut oil
150 g (51/2 oz) minced (ground) pork
75 g (21/2 oz) minced (ground) prawn
   (shrimp) meat
1/2 teaspoon finely chopped makrut
   (kaffir lime) leaves
11/2 tablespoons palm sugar (jaggery)
11/2 tablespoons fish sauce
1 pineapple, quartered, core removed
2 chillies, seeded and finely sliced,
   to garnish

In a blender, put the garlic, coriander root, peppercorns, ginger, spring onions and oil, and pulse until smooth. Heat a frying pan over medium heat, add the paste and cook for 2 minutes. Add the pork and prawn meat and continue to cook, stirring occasionally, until the meat has coloured. Add the makrut leaves, sugar and fish sauce, reduce the heat and cook until the mixture is slightly sticky. Allow to cool. Slice the quartered pineapple into 1 cm (1/2 in) thick triangles, top with the cooled mixture and garnish with chilli.

pistachio and orange crackers

makes 30

125 g (4¹/2 oz/1 cup) plain (all-purpose) flour
45 g (1¹/2 oz/¹/4 cup) rice flour
¹/4 teaspoon baking powder
2 teaspoons chopped orange zest
35 g (1¹/4 oz/¹/4 cup) chopped pistachios
3 tablespoons vegetable oil
100 g (3¹/2 oz/¹/3 cup) plain yoghurt
1 egg white, lightly whisked

Preheat the oven to 180°C (350°F/ Gas 4). Sift the flours, baking powder and 1¹/2 teaspoons of salt into a bowl. Add the orange zest, pistachios and some freshly ground black pepper and mix well. Add the oil and yoghurt and mix to form a dough. Lightly knead until smooth, then put on a floured surface and roll out as thinly as possible. Cut out crackers with a 4 cm (1¹/2 in) round cookie cutter or into 4 cm (1¹/2 in) squares and brush with the egg white. Put onto baking trays lined with baking paper and cook in batches in the oven for 15 minutes or until golden brown. Cool on wire racks. Delicious with a sharp cheddar cheese or with crème fraîche and smoked trout.

goat's cheese tartlets

150 g (5½ oz/1 cup) goat's cheese
250 ml (9 fl oz/1 cup) cream (whipping)
1 egg, beaten
3 egg yolks

filo pastry tart shells
2 ready-made filo pastry sheets
50 g (1¾ oz) butter, melted
thyme leaves, finely chopped

Preheat the oven to 160°C (315°F/ Gas 2–3). Put the two filo sheets onto a clean, dry cutting board. Cut in half lengthways and put one half on top of the other. Cut in half lengthways again and repeat the process until you have a pile of squares approximately 5 x 7 cm (2 x 2¾ in).

Lightly butter three shallow muffin or tart trays. Line each of the moulds with one sheet of filo, pressing the pastry well into the sides. Brush with melted butter and scatter some thyme leaves on top. Cover with a second piece of filo pastry, brush with butter and bake for a few minutes until the pastry is lightly golden. Remove and allow to cool.

Preheat the oven to 180°C (350°F/ Gas 4). Crumble the goat's cheese into a bowl. Slowly add the cream, mashing until the mixture is smooth and creamy. Fold in the egg and egg yolks and season well with salt and freshly ground black pepper. Pour the mix into the tart shells and bake for 12 minutes or until puffed and golden.

chicken and mushroom wontons

4 dried shiitake mushrooms
250 g (9 oz) minced (ground) chicken
4 tablespoons finely chopped bamboo
shoots
2 tablespoons light soy sauce
1 teaspoon finely grated fresh ginger
1/2 teaspoon sesame oil
24 square wonton wrappers
plum sauce (basics), to serve

Soak the shiitake mushrooms in hot water for 30 minutes. Drain the mushrooms, squeeze out any excess moisture and cut off the tough stalks. Finely chop the mushrooms and put them into a bowl with the chicken, bamboo shoots, soy sauce, ginger and sesame oil. Gently stir to combine the filling ingredients.

Put 1 square wonton wrapper on a clean surface and moisten the edge with water. Put 1 heaped teaspoon of the filling mixture into the centre and draw all the edges together. Pinch the edges together to form little bags. Put onto a tray lined with baking paper and repeat with the remaining mixture. Steam for 15 minutes and serve with plum sauce.

chilli corn cakes   makes 24

2 corn cobs
90 g (3 1/4 oz/3/4 cup) plain (all-purpose)
   flour
1 teaspoon baking powder
1 egg
20 g (3/4 oz) melted butter
1/2 teaspoon salt
3 tablespoons milk
1 teaspoon Tabasco sauce
vegetable oil

Remove the kernels from the corn cobs. Put the flour, baking powder, egg, melted butter and salt into a mixing bowl. Stir to combine. Add the milk and Tabasco sauce to form a thick batter, then add the corn and stir through. Heat some vegetable oil in a deep heavy-based frying pan over medium heat. Test if the oil is sizzling hot by dropping in a little batter. Then, drop small spoonfuls of the batter into the oil and fry on each side until golden brown. Remove and drain on paper towel. Serve while still warm.

sweet pork wontons makes 24

300 g (10¹/2 oz) minced (ground) pork
¹/2 teaspoon sea salt
1 teaspoon light soy sauce
1 tablespoon Chinese rice wine
3 spring onions (scallions), finely sliced
¹/2 teaspoon Chinese five-spice
1 teaspoon finely grated fresh ginger
24 square wonton wrappers
peanut oil, for deep-frying
Chinese black vinegar, to serve

Put the pork, sea salt, light soy sauce, Chinese rice wine, spring onions, five-spice and fresh ginger in a bowl. Stir to combine.

Put 1 square wonton wrapper on a clean surface and moisten the edges with a little water. Put 1 heaped teaspoon of the filling mixture in the centre of the wrapper and then fold the wrapper in half to form a triangle. Press to seal the edges, then bring the two pointy ends together over the top of the filling to form a bundle. Put the wontons onto a tray lined with baking paper and repeat with the remaining mixture. To cook, deep-fry in peanut oil and serve with a small dipping bowl of Chinese black vinegar.

corn and prawn pancakes

makes 40 small pancakes

100 g (3½ oz) raw prawn (shrimp) meat
400 g (14 oz/2 cups) corn kernels
2 large eggs
3 tablespoons cornflour (cornstarch)
20 g (¾ oz/⅓ cup) Asian dried shrimp
50 g (1¾ oz/1 cup) chopped coriander
   (cilantro) leaves
2 garlic cloves, minced
2 tablespoons green peppercorns
1 tablespoon sugar
1 tablespoon Worcestershire sauce
125 ml (4 fl oz/½ cup) peanut oil,
   for frying

Put the prawn meat and half of the corn kernels in a food processor and process to a coarse paste. Scrape the paste into a separate bowl and add the rest of the ingredients, except for the oil, mixing well. Heat the oil in a frying pan over moderate heat and cook tablespoons of the mixture in batches, turning the pancakes once until crisp and golden. Serve warm.

whiting and pumpkin tempura

makes 40 pieces

300 g (10¹/₂ oz) jap (kent) pumpkin
  (winter squash), peeled
10 large whiting or firm white fish
  fillets, bones removed
155 g (5¹/₂ oz/1¹/₄ cups) tempura flour
500 ml (17 fl oz/2 cups) canola oil,
  for deep-frying
coriander (cilantro) leaves, to garnish

dipping sauce
2 tablespoons lemon juice
80 ml (2¹/₂ fl oz/¹/₃ cup) soy sauce
2 tablespoons mirin
2 teaspoons pickled ginger juice

Slice the pumpkin into 3 mm (¹/₈ in) slices and set aside. Slice the whiting fillets in half lengthways.

To make the dipping sauce, combine the lemon juice, soy sauce, mirin and pickled ginger juice in a small bowl. Set aside.

Put the tempura flour in a bowl, add 250 ml (9 fl oz/1 cup) of iced water and stir gently with chopsticks until the mixture is just combined and slightly lumpy.

Heat the oil in a wok or deep frying pan over medium heat. Dip the pumpkin slices in the batter and cook in batches for 2–3 minutes, or until lightly golden. Dip the whiting in the batter and cook in batches until lightly golden. Dip the coriander leaves in the batter and cook for a few seconds. Drain all tempura and serve hot, accompanied with the dipping sauce.

artichoke tartlets   makes 20

120 g (4¹/4 oz) bottled artichoke hearts
  in oil, drained
15 garlic cloves, roasted until soft
60 ml (2 fl oz/¹/4 cup) olive oil
¹/2 teaspoon truffle oil
20 pre-baked shortcrust mini tart shells
  (basics)
30 g (1 oz/¹/4 cup) shaved parmesan
  cheese

Put the artichoke hearts, roasted garlic, olive oil and truffle oil in a blender or food processor and blend until smooth. Season according to taste with salt and freshly ground black pepper. Put 1 teaspoon of the mixture into each of the tart shells and top with the shaved parmesan.

fish cakes

makes 24

4 makrut (kaffir lime) leaves, 2 very
  finely sliced
500 g (1 lb 2 oz) salmon fillet
150 g (5 1/2 oz/2 cups) fresh
  breadcrumbs
2 eggs
30 g (1 oz/1/2 cup) spring onions
  (scallions), sliced
2 tablespoons finely chopped
  lemon grass
2 tablespoons finely chopped
  coriander (cilantro) leaves
2 large red chillies, seeded and finely
  chopped
1 tablespoon lime juice
1 teaspoon fish sauce
1/2 teaspoon white pepper
vegetable oil, for frying
lemon wedges, to serve

Put 250 ml (9 fl oz/1 cup) water and 2 whole makrut leaves in a frying pan over high heat. Bring to the boil, then add the salmon fillet and cover. Reduce the heat and simmer for 5 minutes. Remove from the heat.

Using a fork, break up the cooled salmon and put in a large bowl with the fresh breadcrumbs, eggs, 2 finely sliced makrut leaves, spring onions, lemon grass, coriander, chillies, lime juice, fish sauce and white pepper. Stir to combine and then shape into 24 small patties.

Heat some vegetable oil in a non-stick frying pan over medium heat. Cook the fish cakes, in batches, until golden. Serve with lemon wedges.

prawn sandwich

lime mayonnaise
2 egg yolks
1 lime, zested and juiced
250 ml (9 fl oz/1 cup) oil

20 raw prawns (shrimp), peeled and
  deveined
60 ml (2 fl oz/¼ cup) lime juice
60 ml (2 fl oz/¼ cup) light olive oil
2 tablespoons oil, for frying
8 slices white sourdough bread
coriander (cilantro) leaves, to serve
white pepper, to sprinkle

To make the lime mayonnaise, whisk the egg yolks, lime zest and juice in a large bowl. Slowly drizzle in the oil while whisking until the mixture thickens, and keep whisking the mixture until it becomes thick and creamy. Season to taste with sea salt. If the mixture is very thick, add a little cold water until you achieve the right consistency.

Put the prawns, lime juice and light olive oil into a bowl and leave to marinate for half an hour.

Heat some of the oil in a heavy-based frying pan over a high heat. Put a few of the prawns into the pan and sear for about 2 minutes, until they begin to curl. Flip them over and continue to cook for a further minute until they are cooked through. Cook the rest of the prawns, a few at a time, in the same way until all are done.

Spread some lime mayonnaise onto each slice of bread. Divide the prawns between four slices, scatter with coriander leaves and season with white pepper. Top with the remaining bread slices.

tiny brioche
with garlic prawns
makes 36

1 quantity of brioche dough (basics),
  at room temperature
1 egg yolk
1 tablespoon milk
90 g (3¼ oz) butter
3 garlic cloves, crushed
400 g (14 oz) small raw school prawns
  (shrimp), peeled
3 tablespoons lemon juice
1 tablespoon finely chopped flat-leaf
  (Italian) parsley

Grease three mini muffin tins. Break off walnut-sized balls of brioche dough and put them into the moulds. Cover with plastic wrap or a cloth and allow them to rise in a warm place for three hours. Preheat the oven to 180°C (350°F/Gas 4). Make an egg wash by whisking the egg yolk with the milk in a small bowl.

When the dough has doubled in size, glaze the brioche with the egg wash, then bake for 20–30 minutes or until golden brown. Remove from the oven and allow to cool.

Put the butter and garlic into a heavy-based frying pan and cook over moderate heat for 2–3 minutes. Add the prawns and season. Cook for 3 minutes, turning once, then add the lemon juice and parsley. Remove the prawns from the pan, reserving the butter sauce. With a sharp knife, remove the tops of the brioches and scoop out about a teaspoonful of bread from the centre of each to make a deep hole. Fill with the warm prawns and spoon over a little of the butter sauce before replacing the brioche lid.

prawn and water chestnut wontons with plum sauce

serves 36

450 g (1 lb) raw prawns (shrimp),
   chopped, or 210 g (7 1/2 oz) prawn
   (shrimp) meat
90 g (3 1/4 oz/1/2 cup) finely diced
   water chestnuts
60 g (2 1/4 oz/1/2 cup) finely sliced
   spring onions (scallions)
2 tablespoons mirin
1/2 teaspoon sesame oil
2 teaspoons fish sauce
1 egg
36 round wonton wrappers
peanut oil, for deep-frying
plum sauce (basics), to serve

Put the prawn meat, water chestnuts, spring onions, mirin, sesame oil, fish sauce, 1 teaspoon of sea salt and some ground black pepper in a bowl and stir to combine. Beat the egg in a small bowl with 60 ml (2 fl oz/1/4 cup) of water. Put one of the wonton wrappers onto a clean surface and put 1 teaspoon of the prawn mixture in the centre. Brush a little of the egg wash around the edges and bring together, sealing the sides, and twist the top firmly.

Put on a tray lined with baking paper and repeat with the remaining mixture. Heat the oil in a wok or deep frying pan and fry the wontons until they are golden brown. Remove and serve with plum sauce.

fig roll with pecorino

makes 40 slices

250 g (9 oz/1 1/3 cups) finely chopped
   dried figs
2 1/2 teaspoons redcurrant jelly
1 teaspoon brandy
30 g (1 oz/1/4 cup) chopped walnuts
1/4 teaspoon aniseed seeds
6–8 sheets edible rice paper
50 g (1 3/4 oz) pecorino cheese, thinly
   sliced, to serve

Put all the ingredients except the rice paper and pecorino cheese in a food processor and pulse until the mixture begins to clump together. Transfer to a sheet of baking paper and, using the baking paper, roll into a log. Once you have made the log, transfer the log from the baking paper and wrap in edible rice paper. Store covered in a muslin cloth for several days to allow it to dry out. Slice and serve with pecorino cheese.

pickled nectarines with ricotta and prosciutto

makes 24

3 large nectarines (approximately
  500 g/1 lb 2 oz)
150 ml (5 fl oz) cider vinegar
2 star anise
2 cloves
1 teaspoon roughly sliced fresh ginger
1 large red chilli
1 cup caster (superfine) sugar
12 slices prosciutto, cut in half
  lengthways
250 g (9 oz/1 cup) ricotta cheese

Slice the nectarines into quarters, discarding the stones. Put the vinegar, star anise, cloves, ginger, chilli, sugar, 1 pinch of salt and 300 ml (10^1/$_2$ fl oz) of water in a saucepan and bring to the boil. Warm a medium-sized, heat-proof, sealable jar by filling it with boiling water, waiting a few minutes and then draining the water. Put the nectarines in the jar, pour in the boiling vinegar liquid and seal. Cool, then put in the refrigerator for at least 5 days.

To serve, slice the nectarine quarters in half lengthways. Lay the prosciutto slices out on a clean surface and lay one slice of nectarine on top of each. Top with a heaped teaspoon of ricotta cheese and roll up, to serve.

parmesan biscuits
makes 65-70

125 g (4^1/$_2$ oz) butter, chilled and cubed

70 g (2^1/$_2$ oz/^{1}/$_2$ cup) grated cheddar cheese

50 g (1^3/$_4$ oz/^{1}/$_2$ cup) grated parmesan cheese

150 g (5^1/$_2$ oz/1^1/$_2$ cups) plain (all-purpose) flour

1 teaspoon paprika

Put all the ingredients in a food processor with ^{1}/$_4$ teaspoon salt. Using the pulse action, process until the ingredients just combine. Remove the dough and form it into a ball. Divide the dough in half, then roll and shape each portion into a roll about 23 x 3 cm (9 x 1^1/$_4$ in) wide. Roll in baking paper and chill for 1 hour. The dough can be frozen at this point until ready to use.

Preheat the oven to 180°C (350°F/ Gas 4). Remove the baking paper from the dough rolls and cut each portion into 5 mm (^{1}/$_4$ in) slices. Put on a baking tray lined with baking paper and bake for 12–15 minutes, or until pale gold in colour. Cool on a wire rack. Repeat until all the biscuits are cooked. Store in an airtight container until ready to serve.

potato mash

**1 kg (2 lb 4 oz) floury potatoes, peeled
and cut into chunks**
125 ml (4 fl oz/1/2 cup) milk
100 g (31/2 oz) butter

Put the potatoes into a large pot of cold salted water and bring to the boil. Cook for about 30 minutes. Put the milk with the butter into a small saucepan. Warm over low heat until the butter has melted. When the potato is cooked through, drain and return it to the warm pot. Mash while still warm, then whisk in the buttery milk until the potato is soft and creamy. Season according to taste. Spoon into a warm serving bowl and serve immediately. Serve with roasted chicken or grilled (broiled) sausages.

sweet potato, watercress and pear salad

serves 4

1 large orange sweet potato
2 tablespoons olive oil
1 lemon, juiced
1 tablespoon pink peppercorns,
  drained and finely chopped
3 tablespoons extra virgin olive oil
2 ripe green pears, quartered and cut
  into bite-sized pieces
400 g (14 oz) watercress, sprigs picked

Preheat the oven to 180°C (350°F/ Gas 4). Peel and cut the sweet potato into bite-sized chunks and put on a baking tray.

Rub the sweet potato chunks with 2 tablespoons of olive oil and season with sea salt. Bake for 30 minutes, or until they are golden brown and cooked through.

Meanwhile, put the lemon juice, peppercorns and extra virgin olive oil into a large bowl and stir to combine. Add the pear pieces and watercress and toss together. Arrange the pear salad on a serving plate then add the cooked sweet potato.

white bean mash

serves 4

200 g (7 oz/1 cup) cannellini beans
4 garlic cloves
2 teaspoons salt
125 ml (4 fl oz/1/2 cup) olive oil
1 tablespoon thyme leaves

Soak the cannellini beans overnight. Drain the beans and put them into a saucepan with the garlic cloves. Cover generously with cold water and bring to the boil. Reduce the heat and simmer for 1 hour, or until the beans are soft. Stir in 2 teaspoons salt in the last 5 minutes of cooking time. Once the beans are cooked, drain and roughly mash them by hand or in a food processor with the olive oil and thyme leaves. Season to taste with sea salt and freshly ground black pepper. Spoon into a warm serving bowl and serve immediately. Serve with grilled (broiled) sausages or lamb.

asian-style
vegetable salad

serves 6

dressing
1 teaspoon sambal oelek
1 tablespoon finely chopped
   lemon grass
3 tablespoons lime juice
1 tablespoon palm sugar (jaggery)
1 tablespoon finely chopped mint

300 g (10^1/$_2$ oz) French beans, trimmed
   and cut in half
1 red capsicum (pepper), julienned
90 g (3^1/$_4$ oz/1 cup) bean sprouts,
   trimmed
1 Lebanese (short) cucumber, julienned
8 cm (3^1/$_4$ in) piece daikon radish,
   peeled and finely julienned
1 carrot, peeled and finely julienned
40 g (1^1/$_2$ oz/^{1}/$_4$ cup) finely chopped
   roast peanuts

To make the dressing, put the sambal oelek, lemon grass, lime juice, palm sugar and mint into a small bowl and stir to combine. Set aside.

To make the salad, blanch the French beans in boiling water until they are dark green then drain and rinse under running cold water. Put them into a bowl with the remaining ingredients, except the peanuts. Toss together. Pour over the dressing, toss the salad and allow to sit for 15 minutes before serving. Garnish with the peanuts and serve with any simple rice-based Asian-style dish.

sweet couscous   serves 4

175 g (6 oz/1 cup) couscous
3 teaspoons honey
1/2 teaspoon ground cinnamon
1 teaspoon finely grated orange zest
3 tablespoons currants
3 tablespoons toasted flaked almonds
plain yoghurt, to serve

Put the couscous into a saucepan with the honey and 500 ml (17 fl oz/ 2 cups) boiling water. Cover and cook over low heat for 5 minutes, or until all the liquid has been absorbed. Fluff the couscous with a fork, then cover again and remove from the heat. Allow to sit for 10 minutes, then add the cinnamon, orange zest, currants and almonds. Toss to combine and serve with plain yoghurt.

pumpkin mash   serves 4

1 kg (2 lb 4 oz) pumpkin (winter squash)
100 g (3¹/₂ oz) butter
¹/₄ teaspoon ground white pepper
sprinkle of ground cumin
extra virgin olive oil, to drizzle

Peel the pumpkin and cut it into chunks. Put the pumpkin into a large pot of salted cold water and bring to the boil. Boil for 10–12 minutes, or until the pumpkin is cooked through. Drain and return to the pot. Mash while the pumpkin is still warm, then whisk in the butter, white pepper and ground cumin. Season with sea salt. Spoon into a warm serving bowl and drizzle with extra virgin olive oil. Serve with grilled (broiled) lamb or steak.

lemon-braised vegetables

serves 4-6

12 small kipfler (fingerling) potatoes
1 bunch baby carrots, trimmed of tops
6 celery sticks, chopped
125 ml (4 fl oz/1/2 cup) extra virgin
  olive oil
2 lemons, juiced
1 teaspoon sea salt
2 tablespoons finely chopped
  garlic chives

Preheat the oven to 180°C (350°F/ Gas 4). Scrub the potatoes and carrots and remove any blemishes. If the carrots are too large, cut them in half. Put them into a casserole dish with the celery, olive oil, lemon juice, sea salt and 125 ml (4 fl oz/1/2 cup) of water. Cover and put in the oven for 2 hours. When cooked, scatter with the garlic chives. Serve with roast chicken (see page 196) or whole baked fish (see page 171).

celeriac mash

1 kg (2 lb 4 oz) celeriac
2 all-purpose potatoes
1 teaspoon lemon juice
2 garlic cloves
40 g (1¹/2 oz) butter
¹/4 onion, finely diced
125 ml (4 fl oz/¹/2 cup) cream (whipping)

Peel the celeriac and potatoes and cut them into chunks. Put the vegetables into a large saucepan of salted cold water with the lemon juice and garlic. Bring to the boil and cook for 25 minutes, or until the celeriac is soft and you can easily push a knife through it. Drain the vegetables and return them to the pan. Add the butter and onion. Mash while still warm, slowly adding the cream until the mixture is smooth. Season to taste and serve immediately. Serve with grilled (broiled) steak or seared lamb.

mango salsa

1 large or 2 small mangoes
1 spring onion (scallion), finely sliced
1 red chilli, seeded and finely chopped
2 tablespoons lime juice
sesame oil, to sprinkle
1 handful coriander (cilantro) leaves or
   4 large basil leaves, finely sliced
   (optional)

Dice the flesh of the mangoes. Put the mango flesh into a bowl with the onion, chilli, lime juice, sesame oil and some black pepper, to taste. Toss to combine. If you'd like some herbs in this salsa, add the coriander leaves or basil leaves. This salsa adds a lovely summer hit to barbecued prawns (shrimp) or chicken.

jewelled couscous   serves 4

15 saffron threads
20 g (³/4 oz) butter
185 g (6¹/2 oz/1 cup) couscous
75 g (2¹/2 oz/¹/2 cup) currants
60 g (2¹/4 oz/¹/2 cup) slivered almonds, toasted
75 g (2¹/2 oz/¹/2 cup) raw pistachios, toasted
1 orange, zested and juiced
2 tablespoons extra virgin olive oil

Put the saffron threads into a large saucepan with 125 ml (4 fl oz/¹/2 cup) water. Put over a medium heat and cook until the water has reduced by half. Add the butter and couscous and stir to combine. Add 250 ml (9 fl oz/ 1 cup) of boiling water, cover and remove from the heat. After 5 minutes, uncover and fluff the couscous with a fork. Return the lid to the pot and allow to sit for a further 5 minutes.

Put cooked couscous in a bowl and add the currants, almonds, pistachios and orange zest. Toss together and then stir through the orange juice and olive oil. Season with sea salt and freshly ground black pepper. Serve with roast chicken.

mango and coconut chutney

serves 4

90 g (3¹/₄ oz/1 cup) desiccated coconut
1 large green chilli, seeded and roughly
  chopped
1 teaspoon finely grated fresh ginger
1 teaspoon lime juice
100 g (3¹/₂ oz/¹/₃ cup) plain yoghurt
60 g (2¹/₄ oz/¹/₃ cup) finely diced
  mango
2 tablespoons vegetable oil
2 teaspoons mustard seeds
4 small sprigs curry leaves

Put the coconut, chilli and ginger in a food processor and process into a fine paste. Transfer the mixture to a small bowl and add the lime juice, yoghurt and mango.

In a small frying pan, heat the oil over a medium heat and, when hot, add the mustard seeds and curry leaves. When the mustard seeds begin to pop, remove from the heat and spoon the seeds over the coconut mixture. Stir the warm mustard seeds into the coconut mixture and spoon into a small serving bowl. Drain the curry leaves on paper towel and use to garnish the chutney. Serve with grilled prawns or chicken.

yorkshire puddings

makes 12, or 24 mini puddings

125 g (4¹/₂ oz/1 cup) plain
 (all-purpose) flour
¹/₂ teaspoon salt
2 eggs
250 ml (9 fl oz/1 cup) milk

Preheat the oven to 200°C (400°F/ Gas 6). Sift the plain flour into a bowl with the salt. Make a well in the centre and break the eggs into it. Whisk the mixture, slowly adding the milk to form a smooth batter. Transfer the batter into a pouring jug.

Liberally oil two 6-hole muffin tins (or, for mini puddings, two 12-hole muffin tins) and heat the tins in the oven for 15 minutes. Remove from the oven and, working quickly, pour in the batter to half-fill each individual hole. Immediately return to the oven and bake for 25 minutes. Serve with roast beef and gravy.

marinated artichokes   serves 4

4 globe artichokes

3 lemons, halved

60 ml (2 fl oz/¼ cup) extra virgin
   olive oil

8 mint leaves, finely chopped

1 handful flat-leaf (Italian) parsley
   leaves, roughly chopped

1 garlic clove, crushed

Bring a large saucepan of salted water to the boil. Fill a large bowl with cold water and add the juice of 1 lemon. Trim the artichoke stalks to within 2 cm (¾ in) of the artichoke head, then pull away the outer leaves until the base of the leaves look yellow and crisp. Use a sharp knife to slice away the top third of the artichokes and rub the artichoke with the cut side of the lemon. Place in the water and trim the remaining artichokes. Remove the artichokes from the water and scrape out the central choke and pull out any of the spiky inner leaves. Return to the water until ready to cook.

Add the artichokes to the boiling water, weigh them down with a plate and simmer for 20 minutes. Test the artichokes by pushing the tip of a knife just above the stem — it should be tender. Drain, then slice in half.

Put artichokes in a large dish with the olive oil, herbs, garlic and any juice from the remaining lemon. Season with sea salt and freshly ground black pepper and toss to ensure that the artichokes are well coated in the marinade.

boiled eggs roast pumpkin with tahini baked eggs omelette tofu salad with peanut dressing leek, saffron and chickpea soup onion soup poached eggs soba noodles with ginger broth sweet onion and herb tart barley and bacon soup soba noodle salad miso broth with somen noodles, shiitake and pumpkin spring chowder crab and tomato tart shiitake mushroom, pumpkin and tofu duck and noodle soup quiche lorraine

02 light meals

tamarind and squid salad gruyère baked eggs duck and mango rolls mustard rubbed tuna salad soba noodle and herb salad asparagus and broad bean boiled eggs roast pumpkin with tahini baked eggs omelette tofu salad with peanut dressing leek soup

boiled eggs

2 eggs
buttered toast soldiers, to serve

Take the eggs from the refrigerator and allow to come to room temperature. Fill a small saucepan with enough cold water to cover the eggs and bring it to the boil over high heat. When it has reached boiling point, reduce the heat to a rolling boil. Using a spoon, lower the eggs, one at a time, into the water. Boil for 5 minutes, then remove. If you prefer your eggs set firmly, then cook for a further 1 minute. Perch each egg in an egg cup and, with a sharp knife, crack off the top. Serve with sea salt, pepper and buttered toast soldiers.

roast pumpkin with tahini

serves 4

900 g (2 lb) butternut pumpkin (squash)
1 tablespoon oil
3 tablespoons tahini
125 g (4^1/$_2$ oz/^{1}/$_2$ cup) plain yoghurt
1 teaspoon ground roast cumin
^{1}/$_2$ teaspoon finely chopped garlic
1 tablespoon lemon juice
120 g (4^1/$_4$ oz/3^1/$_2$ cups) rocket
  (arugula)
1 large handful flat-leaf (Italian)
  parsley leaves
1 tablespoon black sesame seeds

Preheat the oven to 180°C (350°F/ Gas 4). Peel the pumpkin and cut it into large chunks. Toss it in the oil, season with sea salt and freshly ground black pepper and then put the chunks on a baking tray. Roast for 30 minutes or until the pumpkin is tender, then allow it to cool.

To make the dressing, mix the tahini, yoghurt, cumin, garlic and lemon juice to a smooth paste and then season with sea salt and pepper to taste.

Toss the rocket and parsley leaves together and pile them onto a serving plate. Top with the roast pumpkin, add a spoonful of the dressing and then garnish with a sprinkling of black sesame seeds.

baked eggs

4 eggs
1 tablespoon finely snipped chives
**2 tablespoons finely grated parmesan
  cheese**
ground white pepper

Preheat the oven to 180°C (350°F/ Gas 4). Generously grease two 8 cm (3¼ in) ramekins and put them in a roasting tin half-filled with water. Put the eggs into a small bowl and add the chives and parmesan cheese. Whisk together and season with sea salt and ground white pepper. Divide the egg mixture between the two ramekins and bake for 15 minutes, or until the egg is cooked through. Serve with hot toast.

omelette

3 eggs
20 g (3/4 oz) butter
baby English spinach leaves, to garnish
chives, snipped, to garnish

Separate the eggs. Whisk the egg whites until they form soft peaks, then lightly fold the egg yolks and whites together.

Heat a 25 cm (10 in) non-stick frying pan over medium heat and add the butter. When the butter has melted and begins to sizzle, pour in the egg mixture. Using a spatula, fold the edges of the egg into the centre as it cooks.

When the egg is nearly cooked, flip one side of the omelette over the other and remove the pan from the heat. Gently slide the cooked omelette onto a plate. Serve with the baby spinach on the side and garnish with a sprinkling of snipped chives.

tofu salad with
peanut dressing

1 tablespoon shaved palm sugar
(jaggery)
5 tablespoons boiling water
1 tablespoon balsamic vinegar
2 tablespoons kecap manis
1 red chilli, seeded and finely chopped
1 garlic clove, finely chopped
70 g (2¹/2 oz/¹/2 cup) roasted and
ground peanuts
300 g (10¹/2 oz) hard tofu, cut into 2 cm
(³/4 in) cubes
90 g (3¹/4 oz/¹/2 cup) rice flour
300 ml (10¹/2 fl oz) peanut oil
60 g (2¹/4 oz/2 cups) watercress sprigs
90 g (3¹/4 oz/1 cup) bean sprouts,
trimmed

To make the dressing, combine the palm sugar, boiling water, vinegar and kecap manis in a small bowl. Stir until the palm sugar has dissolved. Add the chilli, garlic and peanuts. Set aside.
Drain the tofu on paper towel and cut into small cubes. Put the rice flour into a plastic bag with a little sea salt and freshly ground black pepper. Add the tofu and toss until well coated. Heat a frying pan over a high heat and add the peanut oil. Deep-fry several tofu cubes at a time until they are golden brown, then remove with a slotted spoon and drain on paper towel. To assemble the salad, arrange the watercress and bean sprouts on four plates and top with the tofu. Drizzle with the dressing.

leek, saffron and chickpea soup

serves 4

40 g (1 1/2 oz) butter
15 saffron threads
3 leeks, white part only, finely diced
1 lemon, zest peeled into thick strips
1 carrot, peeled and grated
3 tablespoons roughly chopped
  flat-leaf (Italian) parsley
1 litre (35 fl oz/4 cups) chicken stock
  (basics)
400 g (14 oz) tin chickpeas, drained
  and rinsed

Heat the butter and saffron threads in a large saucepan over medium heat. Add the leeks when the butter begins to bubble and cook until they are soft and transparent. Add the lemon zest, carrot and parsley and cook for a further minute before adding the stock and chickpeas. Bring to the boil then reduce the heat and simmer for a further 15 minutes. Serve hot.

onion soup

serves 4

40 g (1 1/2 oz) butter
8 onions, peeled and finely sliced
2 garlic cloves
1 tablespoon finely chopped rosemary
1 litre (35 fl oz/4 cups) chicken stock
   (basics)
ground white pepper
30 g (1 oz/1 cup) roughly chopped
   flat-leaf (Italian) parsley
70 g (2 1/2 oz/2/3 cup) grated vintage
   cheddar cheese

Melt the butter in a large saucepan over a medium heat and then add the onions, garlic and rosemary. Cover and allow the onions to slowly sauté, stirring occasionally until they are soft and have almost dissolved. This will take about half an hour.

Add the chicken stock, season with sea salt and ground white pepper and continue to cook for a further half hour. To serve, divide the soup between four large soup bowls and sprinkle the parsley and cheese on top. Serve immediately.

poached eggs

1 egg
1 teaspoon white wine vinegar
wholemeal toast, to serve

For great poached eggs, really fresh eggs are essential. Fill a deep frying pan with about 5 cm (2 in) cold water. Add white wine vinegar and bring to a simmering boil. Crack an egg into a saucer and gently lower the egg into the water. Lower the heat and cook for 5 minutes. Remove the egg with a slotted spoon and drain on a paper towel. Serve with wholemeal toast.

soba noodles
with ginger broth
serves 4

400 g (14 oz) buckwheat (soba)
  noodles
1 litre (35 fl oz/4 cups) chicken stock
  (basics)
1 tablespoon finely grated fresh ginger
2 teaspoons soy sauce
1 teaspoon fish sauce
3 spring onions (scallions), finely sliced
300 g (10½ oz) fresh soft tofu, cut into
  2 cm (¾ in) cubes

Bring a large pot of water to the boil and cook the noodles until they are *al dente*. Drain and rinse under cold running water and set aside. Put the stock, ginger, soy sauce and fish sauce into a saucepan and bring to the boil. Reduce the heat to low and allow to simmer for 5 minutes.

Divide the noodles between four bowls and top with the spring onion and tofu. Ladle the hot broth over the noodles and serve immediately.

sweet onion and herb tart

serves 6

30 g (1 oz) butter
1/2 teaspoon finely chopped rosemary
1/2 teaspoon finely chopped thyme
800 g (1 lb 12 oz) onions, finely sliced
125 ml (4 fl oz/1/2 cup) white wine
1 pre-baked 25 cm (10 in) shortcrust
  tart case (basics)
250 ml (9 fl oz/1 cup) thick
  (double/heavy) cream
4 egg yolks
70 g (21/2 oz/1/2 cup) grated gruyère
  cheese

Preheat the oven to 180°C (350°F/ Gas 4). Using a large frying pan (with a lid), melt the butter over medium heat along with the rosemary and thyme. Add the onions and sauté until the onion is soft and transparent. Add the white wine and cover the pan. Reduce the heat and gently simmer for 40 minutes, or until the onion is richly caramelized. Spread the onion mixture into the tart case.

Put the cream into a bowl with the egg yolks and whisk together. Season with sea salt and freshly ground black pepper and stir in the gruyère cheese. Pour the cream mixture over the onion and carefully put the tart into the oven. Bake for 30 minutes, or until the filling has set and is lightly golden. Serve with a bitter leaf salad.

barley and bacon soup serves 4

40 g (1 1/2 oz) butter
2 garlic cloves, minced
3 leeks, white part only, washed and
  finely chopped
1 teaspoon thyme leaves
1/2 teaspoon finely chopped rosemary
4 slices bacon, finely diced
1 large carrot, grated
2 celery sticks, finely sliced
175 g (6 oz) pearl barley
2 litres (70 fl oz/8 cups) chicken or
  vegetable stock (basics)
1 handful flat-leaf (Italian) parsley
  leaves
50 g (1 3/4 oz/1/2 cup) grated
  parmesan cheese

Melt the butter in a large saucepan over a medium heat and add the garlic and leeks. Stir for 1 minute before adding the thyme, rosemary and bacon. Continue to cook until the leeks are soft and transparent. Add the carrot, celery and barley and cook for a further 5 minutes, stirring. Pour in the stock, cover with a lid and reduce the heat to a simmer. Cook for 1 hour, or until the barley is soft.

Ladle the hot soup into four bowls and top with the parsley leaves and parmesan cheese.

soba noodle salad   serves 4

4 tablespoons arame or hijiki
1 teaspoon dashi granules
125 ml (4 fl oz/1/2 cup) soy sauce
60 ml (2 fl oz/1/4 cup) mirin
1 teaspoon sugar
4 spring onions (scallions), finely sliced
  on the diagonal
300 g (101/2 oz) buckwheat (soba)
  noodles
1 tablespoon pickled ginger, finely
  chopped
500 g (1 lb 2 oz) daikon, julienned
1 Lebanese (short) cucumber, julienned
20 mint leaves, roughly torn

Soak the arame in warm water for 30 minutes and then drain it. Combine the dashi granules, soy sauce, mirin and sugar with 375 ml (13 fl oz/ 11/2 cups) of water in a small saucepan and bring to the boil, stirring so that the sugar dissolves. Remove from the heat and allow the sauce to cool. Add the pickled ginger and spring onions.

Cook the noodles in a pot of boiling water until they are *al dente*, then drain them and rinse with cold water to remove any starch.

Toss the noodles, daikon, arame, cucumber, mint and sauce together and divide between four bowls. Serve the salad as is, or top it with a small piece of teriyaki salmon.

miso broth with somen noodles, shiitake and pumpkin

serves 4

6 dried shiitake mushrooms
1 teaspoon dashi granules
3 tablespoons miso paste
2 tablespoons soy sauce
300 g (10¹/₂ oz) pumpkin (winter
   squash), peeled and cut into 2 cm
   (³/₄ in) cubes
200 g (7 oz) somen noodles
2 spring onions (scallions), sliced
   diagonally

Cover the mushrooms with 500 ml (17 fl oz/2 cups) hot water and soak for about 30 minutes. Remove and finely slice the mushrooms, reserving the soaking liquid.

Put the dashi granules, 1 litre (35 fl oz/ 4 cups) water, the reserved mushroom liquid, miso paste, soy sauce, sliced mushrooms and pumpkin into a large saucepan and bring to the boil. Reduce the heat and simmer for 10 minutes.

Bring a large pot of water to the boil and cook the somen noodles for 3 minutes. Drain, rinse and divide among four warm bowls. Spoon the miso soup over the noodles and top with the sliced spring onion.

spring chowder

1.5 kg (3 lb 5 oz) cleaned clams
  (vongole)
1 tablespoon light olive oil
1 garlic clove, crushed
2 slices bacon, chopped
2 onions, diced
1 red chilli, seeded and finely chopped
1 carrot, grated
1 bay leaf
2 large all-purpose potatoes, peeled
  and diced
2 celery sticks, thinly sliced
30 g (1 oz/1 cup) roughly chopped
  flat-leaf (Italian) parsley
white pepper

Throw away any clams that don't close when you tap them. Bring 500 ml (17 fl oz/2 cups) of water to the boil in a large saucepan, add the clams, then cover and cook for 2–3 minutes until they open. Discard any that stay closed. Take most of the clams out of their shells, keeping some whole for garnish. Strain and reserve the clam liquid.

Put the olive oil, garlic and bacon in the saucepan and cook over a medium heat until the bacon has browned. Add the onions, chilli, carrot and bay leaf. When the onion is translucent, tip in the potatoes, clam liquid and 250 ml (9 fl oz/1 cup) of water. Cover and simmer for 35 minutes. Add the celery, clams and parsley. Season with salt and white pepper. Ladle the chowder into four soup bowls and garnish with whole clams.

crab and tomato tart   serves 6

10 saffron threads
250 ml (9 fl oz/1 cup) thick
  (double/heavy) cream
4 egg yolks
3 tablespoons finely snipped chives
1 pre-baked 25 cm (10 in) shortcrust
  tart case (basics)
2 ripe roma (plum) tomatoes, finely
  chopped
150 g (5$\frac{1}{2}$ oz) fresh crab meat,
  shredded

Preheat the oven to 180°C (350°F/ Gas 4). Put the saffron threads in a small saucepan with 4 tablespoons cold water. Place over high heat and simmer until the liquid has reduced to approximately 1 tablespoon. Remove from the heat and add the cream. Stir to combine, then whisk in the egg yolks. Season with sea salt and freshly ground black pepper and then add the chives. Scatter the tomato in the pre-baked tart case. Scatter the crab meat over the tomato. Pour the cream mixture over the tomato and crab. Bake the tart for 25 minutes, or until the filling has set and is lightly golden. Serve with a watercress salad.

shiitake mushroom, pumpkin and tofu

serves 2

300 g (10½ oz) silken firm tofu, at room
  temperature
6 dried shiitake mushrooms
2 cm (¾ in) fresh ginger, peeled and
  cut into thin strips
250 g (9 oz) daikon, peeled and cut
  into 1 cm (½ in) rounds
100 g (3½ oz) carrot, peeled and cut
  into 1 cm (½ in) rounds
500 g (1 lb 2 oz) pumpkin (winter
  squash), peeled and cut into large
  chunks

Put the shiitake mushrooms into 500 ml (17 fl oz/2 cups) hot water to soak for 30 minutes. Remove the mushrooms and trim off any tough stems. Put the mushrooms in a saucepan along with the strained soaking liquid and add the ginger, daikon and carrot. Bring to the boil, then reduce the heat and simmer for 10 minutes. Add the pumpkin pieces and allow to gently simmer, covered for a further 20–25 minutes.

Cut the tofu into large chunks and divide between two warmed bowls. Check that the pumpkin is cooked through with the point of a sharp knife, then spoon the hot ingredients and stock into the bowls. Serve immediately.

duck and noodle soup serves 4

2 duck breasts, trimmed, reserving
   excess fat
8 spring onions (scallions), sliced into
   3 cm (1¹/₄ in) lengths
250 g (9 oz) buckwheat (soba) noodles
1.5 litres (52 fl oz/6 cups) dashi stock
   (basics)
4 tablespoons soy sauce
1 tablespoon sugar

Finely slice the meat across the duck breast in 5 mm (¹/₄ in) thick slices. Heat the duck fat in a frying pan, add the spring onions and sauté lightly, then set aside.

Cook the noodles in boiling water, drain and set aside. Combine the dashi stock, soy sauce and sugar in a saucepan and bring to the boil. Reduce the heat and simmer for 10 minutes. Add the sliced duck and cook for a further 1 minute.

Divide the noodles among four warmed bowls. Top the noodles with the duck meat and sautéed spring onion. Ladle the hot duck broth into each bowl and serve.

quiche lorraine

1 teaspoon butter
6 slices bacon, finely chopped
2 eggs
2 egg yolks
250 ml (9 fl oz/1 cup) thick
  (double/heavy) cream
white pepper
100 g (3¹/₂ oz/1 cup) grated parmesan
  cheese
1 pre-baked 25 cm (10 in) tart case
  (basics)

Preheat the oven to 180°C (350°F/ Gas 4). Melt the butter in a heavy-based frying pan over medium heat. Add the bacon to the pan and cook until lightly brown and crisp. Remove with a slotted spoon and drain on paper towel.

Put the eggs, egg yolks and cream into a bowl and whisk together. Season with sea salt and white pepper, then stir in the parmesan cheese. Scatter the bacon in the pre-baked tart case and pour the cream mixture over it. Carefully put the tart into the oven and bake for 25 minutes, or until the filling is set and the top golden brown. Serve with a green salad.

tamarind and squid salad

serves 4

1 tablespoon tamarind concentrate
1 tablespoon sugar
2 tablespoons fish sauce
1 tablespoon lime juice
1 garlic clove, crushed
1 small red chilli, seeded and julienned
4 medium squid (about 400 g/14 oz),
    cleaned
3 tablespoons oil
15 g (^{1}/2 oz/^{1}/2 cup) basil leaves
15 g (^{1}/2 oz/^{1}/2 cup) coriander (cilantro)
    leaves
90 g (3^1/4 oz/1 cup) bean sprouts

To make the dressing, blend the tamarind with 60 ml (2 fl oz/^{1}/4 cup) of warm water, add the sugar, fish sauce, lime juice, garlic and chilli and stir until the sugar has dissolved.

Rinse the squid under cold running water and pat it dry with paper towel. Cut the tubes open down one side and lightly criss-cross the outside surface of the squid with score marks to make it curl up when you cook it. Heat the oil in a frying pan over a high heat and fry the squid tubes for 3–4 minutes on each side.

Cut each tube into bite-size pieces and toss them in the dressing with the herbs and sprouts. Serve with steamed white rice or rice noodles.

gruyère baked eggs   makes 4

40 g (1 1/2 oz) butter, softened
4 slices prosciutto, finely chopped
4 tablespoons finely chopped flat-leaf
  (Italian) parsley
8 eggs
2 tablespoons grated gruyère cheese
toast, to serve

Preheat the oven to 180°C (350°F/ Gas 4). Generously butter four 8 cm (3 1/4 in) ramekins and put them into a roasting tin half-filled with water.

Divide the prosciutto and parsley between the ramekins. Put the eggs in a bowl, season with salt and pepper, and then lightly whisk them together. Fill the ramekins with the egg mix, sprinkle with the cheese and put the roasting tin into the oven. Bake for 25–30 minutes, by which time the egg should be just set. Serve with toast.

duck and mango rolls   serves 4

1 teaspoon sichuan peppercorns
1 teaspoon black peppercorns
1/2 teaspoon sea salt
1/2 Chinese roasted duck
8 round rice paper wrappers
4 tablespoons plum sauce (basics)
2 ripe mangoes, peeled and sliced
50 g (1 3/4 oz) snowpea (mangetout)
  shoots

Put both types of peppercorn and the sea salt into a spice grinder and grind to form a coarse seasoning. Set aside. Remove the skin from the duck and slice it into thin strips with a pair of clean kitchen scissors. Remove the flesh and shred it.

Soak the rice paper wrappers in hot water, one at a time, until they become soft, then remove them and pat dry.

Put some of the plum sauce along the centre of a softened wrapper and top with some duck flesh, duck skin, sliced mango, snowpea shoots and a sprinkle of the seasoning. Roll up, folding in the sides to make a neat parcel. When ready to serve, cut the parcels in half and arrange on a serving platter.

mustard rubbed tuna salad

serves 4

1 teaspoon ground white pepper
1 tablespoon dijon mustard
3 tablespoons olive oil
400 g (14 oz) tuna fillet, cut into
  2 cm (3/4 in) square lengths
400 g (14 oz) watercress, leaves picked
70 g (21/2 oz) chervil, trimmed
2 small zucchini (courgettes), finely
  sliced
4 red radishes, finely sliced
125 g (41/2 oz/1/2 cup) lemon
  mayonnaise (basics)

Mix the white pepper, dijon mustard and 1 tablespoon of olive oil together in a small bowl. Rub the mustard mixture all over the tuna.

Add the remaining olive oil to a large non-stick frying pan and heat over a high heat. Sear the tuna for 1 minute on each side. Remove from the heat and allow to rest. Divide the watercress, chervil, zucchini and radish between four plates.

Cut the tuna fillet into thin slices and arrange over the salad. Top with a dollop of lemon mayonnaise.

soba noodle
and herb salad

serves 4

3 tablespoons soy sauce

3 tablespoons sesame oil

1 1/2 tablespoons Chinese black vinegar

3 tablespoons grated palm sugar
  (jaggery)

3 tablespoons lime juice

1 tablespoon finely chopped
  lemon grass, white part only

1 red chilli, seeded and finely chopped

300 g (10 1/2 oz) buckwheat (soba)
  noodles

5 cm (2 in) piece fresh ginger, peeled
  and finely julienned

80 g (2 3/4 oz/about 1 bunch) mint

90 g (3 1/4 oz/about 1 bunch) coriander
  (cilantro)

12 cm (4 1/2 in) piece daikon, peeled
  and julienned

Put the soy sauce, sesame oil, vinegar, sugar, lime juice, lemon grass and chilli into a large bowl and stir until the sugar has dissolved.

Bring a large pot of water to the boil and cook the noodles until *al dente*, then drain and rinse them under cold running water. Put them in the bowl with the dressing and toss to coat the noodles. Add the ginger, mint, coriander and daikon to the noodles, toss together, then pile into four bowls, to serve.

asparagus and broad bean salad

serves 4

3 tablespoons extra virgin olive oil
1 tablespoon lemon juice
2 bunches asparagus, trimmed
300 g (10 1/2 oz/1 3/4 cups) broad (fava) beans
100 g (3 1/2 oz/2/3 cup) goat's cheese
1 handful of flat-leaf (Italian) parsley

Bring a large pot of salted water to the boil. Put the olive oil and lemon juice into a large bowl and season with sea salt and freshly ground black pepper. Add the asparagus to the boiling water and cook for a few minutes until emerald green. Remove from the water with tongs and rinse under cold running water.

Put the asparagus into the bowl with the lemon juice and oil and toss so that the asparagus is well coated in the dressing. Add the broad beans to the boiling water and cook for 5 minutes. Drain and remove the tough outer skin. Divide the asparagus between 4 plates and scatter with the broad beans. Top with the goat's cheese and parsley leaves and drizzle with any of the leftover dressing.

leek and lemon fettucine whole baked fish salmon
with lemon grass and black vinegar dressing leek and
pumpkin risotto roast pumpkin and onions on couscous
with harissa braised mushrooms with buttered angel
hair pasta blue-eye cod with white pepper and lemon
sauce roast lamb couscous with herbs and chickpeas
somen noodles with seared prawns zucchini and thyme
risotto snapper with citrus dressing tuna salad with

03   mains

fried lemon zest hokkien noodle stir-fry lemon thyme
roast chicken pan-fried fish fillets with lemon and
black bean sauce lemon pasta seared lime salmon with
poppy seeds aromatic noodles with seared salmon
steamed fish with fresh ginger lemon and saffron

leek and lemon fettucine

serves 4

3 tablespoons olive oil
3 garlic cloves, crushed
1 tablespoon oregano leaves
3 large leeks, white part only, finely
  sliced
400 g (14 oz) fettucine
1 lemon, zest grated
1 tablespoon small capers
70 g (2½ oz/¾ cup) grated parmesan
  cheese
30 g (1 oz/1 cup) roughly chopped
  flat-leaf (Italian) parsley
grated parmesan cheese, extra,
  to serve

Bring a large saucepan of water to the boil for the pasta. Heat the olive oil in a large frying pan over a medium heat and then add the minced garlic, oregano and leeks. Sauté until the leeks are soft and transparent, then season with sea salt and freshly ground black pepper.

Cook the pasta until it is *al dente*, then drain and return it to the warm pan. Add the leeks, grated lemon zest, capers, parmesan cheese and parsley, stirring them into the pasta. Season with salt and freshly ground black pepper, then serve with extra parmesan cheese.

whole baked fish serves 4

2 lemon grass stems, white part only,
  roughly chopped
1 large piece of ginger, thickly sliced
3 spring onions (scallions), cut into
  4 cm (1 1/2 in) lengths
250 ml (9 fl oz/1 cup) white wine
1.5 kg (3 lb 5 oz) whole snapper, or
  other firm white fish
1 lemon grass stem, white part only,
  finely sliced, extra
1 lemon, thickly sliced
2 tablespoons olive oil
lemon wedges, extra, to serve

Put the 2 chopped lemon grass stems, ginger and spring onion into a roasting tin. Pour over the white wine. Rinse the fish under cold running water and pat dry with paper towel. Using a sharp knife, cut the fish skin in a crisscross pattern. Rub the fish with a little sea salt and put into the roasting tin. Put the finely sliced lemon grass stem and the lemon into the fish cavity. Lightly drizzle the fish with olive oil and bake for 35–40 minutes. Serve with lemon wedges.

salmon with lemon grass and black vinegar dressing

serves 4

black vinegar dressing
1 lemon grass stem
1 tablespoon finely grated fresh ginger
125 ml (4 fl oz/1/2 cup) mirin
2 tablespoons Chinese black vinegar

500 g (1 lb 2 oz/1 bunch) English spinach, washed and trimmed
4 spring onions (scallions), trimmed and cut into 3 cm (11/4 in) lengths
4 x 180 g (6 oz) salmon fillets

To make the lemon grass and black vinegar dressing, trim the lemon grass stem of its tough outer leaves and base. Slice the stem in half lengthways and finely chop the tender bottom 3 cm (11/4 in). Put in a small bowl with the ginger, mirin and vinegar.

Put the English spinach leaves and spring onions in a large frying pan. Add 250 ml (9 fl oz/1 cup) of water and top with the salmon. Put over a high heat and cover so that the water begins to steam the spinach. Cook for a further 8 minutes.

Remove the salmon carefully and put onto warmed plates with the spinach and spring onions. Spoon over the dressing. Season with freshly ground black pepper.

leek and pumpkin risotto

serves 4

1 litre (35 fl oz/4 cups) chicken or
  vegetable stock (basics)
40 g (1½ oz) butter
800 g (1 lb 12 oz) jap (kent) pumpkin
  (winter squash), peeled and finely
  diced
2 leeks, white part only, finely sliced
2 garlic cloves, finely chopped
225 g (8 oz/1 cup) arborio (risotto) rice
4 tablespoons grated parmesan
  cheese, plus extra to serve
olive oil, to drizzle

Heat the stock in a saucepan. In another heavy-based saucepan, heat the butter over medium heat. Add the garlic and leeks. Sauté until the leek is soft. Add the rice and stir for 1 minute, or until the grains are well coated and glossy. Add 250 ml (9 fl oz/1 cup) stock, simmer and stir until absorbed. Add the diced pumpkin and another 250 ml (9 fl oz/1 cup) stock and stir until absorbed. Add 250 ml (9 fl oz/ 1 cup) stock, stir until absorbed, then test if the rice is *al dente*. If the rice is undercooked, add the remaining stock and simmer until the stock has reduced and the rice is coated in a creamy sauce. Fold the parmesan cheese through.

Spoon into bowls and sprinkle with more cheese. Garnish with a drizzle of olive oil.

roast pumpkin and onions on couscous with harissa

serves 4

800 g (1 lb 12 oz) pumpkin (winter squash), cut into large bite-sized pieces
6 small spring onions (scallions), trimmed and halved
2 tablespoons extra virgin olive oil
185 g (6^1/$_2$ oz/1 cup) couscous
375 ml (13 fl oz/1^1/$_2$ cups) boiling water
20 g (^{3}/$_4$ oz) butter
50 g (1^3/$_4$ oz/1 cup) baby English spinach leaves
harissa (basics)

Preheat the oven to 200°C (400°F/ Gas 6). Put the pumpkin pieces and spring onions into a baking dish. Drizzle with olive oil and season with sea salt and freshly ground black pepper. Bake for 20 minutes. Remove from the oven and turn the pumpkin and onions over. Return to the oven and bake for a further 20 minutes.

In a bowl, cover the couscous with boiling water and add the butter. Cover the bowl and allow to sit for 5 minutes. Fluff the couscous with a fork and then spoon onto four plates. Top with the spinach leaves, pumpkin and onions and then spoon over the harissa.

braised mushrooms with buttered angel hair pasta

700 g (1 lb 9 oz) mixed mushrooms (button, Swiss brown, shiitake, oyster and enoki)
3 tablespoons olive oil
3 garlic cloves, crushed
1 tablespoon thyme leaves
250 ml (9 fl oz/1 cup) white wine
250 g (9 oz) fresh angel hair pasta or dried linguine
40 g (1 1/2 oz) butter
2 tablespoons finely chopped flat-leaf (Italian) parsley
4 tablespoons finely grated parmesan cheese

Bring a large pot of salted water to the boil. Cut the mushrooms into halves or quarters. Heat the oil in a large saucepan over a medium heat and add the garlic, mushrooms and thyme. Toss the mushrooms in the pan and cook until the garlic begins to soften. Add the white wine and season with sea salt. Cover with a lid and simmer for 7 minutes.

Add the pasta to the boiling water and cook until *al dente*. Drain the pasta then put it back in the hot saucepan. Stir the butter and parsley through the pasta then pile onto four warmed plates. Make a well in the centre of the pasta and fill with the mushrooms. Drizzle with the mushroom cooking liquid and season with freshly ground black pepper. Serve sprinkled with the parmesan cheese.

blue-eye cod with white pepper and lemon sauce

serves 4

2 lemons, juiced
1 teaspoon ground white pepper
1 teaspoon caster (superfine) sugar
4 x 200 g (7 oz) blue-eye cod or
    firm white fish fillets
2 tablespoons olive oil
3 tomatoes, roughly chopped
12 basil leaves

To make the white pepper and lemon sauce, put the lemon juice, white pepper and sugar into a small bowl and stir until the sugar has dissolved. Rinse the fish fillets in cold water and dry on paper towel.

Heat the olive oil in a large non-stick frying pan over a high heat. Add the fillets and cook for 2 minutes on one side. Turn the fish over and reduce the heat to low–medium. Cook for a further 3–4 minutes.

Toss the tomato and basil together and divide between four plates. Arrange the fish over the top and spoon over the dressing. Serve with a rocket (arugula) salad.

roast lamb

serves 6

1.5 kg (3 lb 5 oz) leg of lamb
olive oil
5 garlic cloves, halved
6 rosemary sprigs

Preheat the oven to 200°C (400°F/ Gas 6). With the point of a small sharp knife, make several incisions into the skin of the leg of lamb. Rub the surface of the lamb with a little olive oil and then rub salt and pepper into the skin. Press the garlic into the incisions. Scatter rosemary over the base of a roasting tin and put the lamb on top.

Bake for 30 minutes, then spoon some of the juices from the tin over the lamb. Bake for 40 minutes. Transfer the lamb to a warm platter, cover with aluminium foil and rest it for 15 minutes before carving. Serve with roasted vegetables.

couscous with herbs and chickpeas

serves 4

185 g (6$^{1}/_{2}$ oz/1 cup) couscous

1 teaspoon butter

400 g (14 oz/1$^{3}/_{4}$ cups) tin chickpeas, drained and rinsed

2 roma (plum) tomatoes, seeded and diced

$^{1}/_{2}$ red onion, finely diced

1 large handful mint leaves

1 large handful coriander (cilantro) leaves

1 large handful flat-leaf (Italian) parsley leaves

1 tablespoon lemon juice

3 tablespoons olive oil

2 tablespoons diced preserved lemon

Put the couscous in a large bowl with the butter and cover with 250 ml (9 fl oz/1 cup) of boiling water. Leave the couscous for 20–30 minutes, from time to time separating the grains with a fork. Before adding the remaining salad ingredients, rub the grains between your fingers to break up any lumps.

Toss the couscous and salad together and season with sea salt and freshly ground black pepper.

somen noodles with seared prawns

serves 4

3 tablespoons rice vinegar
1 teaspoon finely grated fresh ginger
60 ml (2 fl oz/¼ cup) sweet mirin
1 tablespoon tamari
150 g (5½ oz) somen noodles
1 tablespoon olive oil
16 large raw prawns (shrimp), peeled
  and deveined with tails intact
2 Lebanese (short) cucumbers, finely
  julienned
30 g (1 oz/⅔ cup) finely snipped
  chives
2 tablespoons raw sesame seeds
1 teaspoon red chilli flakes

Put the rice vinegar, ginger, mirin and tamari into a small bowl and stir to combine. Set aside.

In a pot of boiling water cook the noodles until they are *al dente*. Rinse the noodles and set aside.

Heat a non-stick frying pan over a high heat and add the olive oil. Sear the prawns on both sides for about 2–3 minutes, or until they are pink and beginning to curl up. Put the noodles into a bowl with the dressing, cucumber and chives. Stir to combine then divide between four bowls. Top with the seared prawns.

Put the sesame seeds and chilli flakes into a shallow saucepan and cook over a medium heat, stirring lightly, until the seeds begin to turn golden brown. Spoon the warm seeds over the top of the prawns and drizzle with any remaining dressing.

zucchini and thyme risotto

serves 4

1 litre (35 fl oz/4 cups) chicken or
  vegetable stock (basics)
60 g (2¼ oz) butter
2 garlic cloves, chopped
1 onion, finely diced
3 zucchini (courgettes), finely diced
1 tablespoon thyme
225 g (8 oz/1 cup) arborio (risotto) rice
250 ml (9 fl oz/1 cup) white wine
70 g (2½ oz/¾ cup) grated parmesan
  cheese
goat's cheese, to serve
drizzle of olive oil, to serve

Heat the chicken or vegetable stock in
a saucepan. Heat 1 tablespoon butter
in a large frying pan over medium heat,
then add the garlic, onion and
zucchini. Sauté until soft and set aside.
Heat 2 tablespoons of butter and the
thyme in a heavy-based saucepan
over medium heat. Add the rice and
stir for 1 minute, or until the grains are
coated. Add the wine, simmer and stir
until absorbed. Add 250 ml (9 fl oz/
1 cup) stock and stir until absorbed.
Stir in another 250 ml (9 fl oz/1 cup)
stock. When nearly all absorbed, stir
in the zucchini. Test if the rice is *al
dente*. If undercooked, add the
remaining stock and simmer until the
stock has reduced and the rice is
coated with the sauce. Fold the
parmesan cheese through. Spoon
into four bowls. Garnish with goat's
cheese and a drizzle of olive oil.

snapper with citrus dressing

serves 4

2 oranges
1 lemon
2 limes
1/2 teaspoon pink peppercorns, roughly
  chopped
4 tablespoons light olive oil
2 tablespoons oil
4 x 200 g (7 oz) snapper or firm white
  fish fillets, skin on

Preheat the oven to 200°C (400°F/ Gas 6). To make the dressing, zest the oranges, lemon and limes and put the zest into a bowl. Juice the lemon and add the juice to the bowl. Segment the oranges and limes and put them in the bowl along with any juice, then add the peppercorns and light olive oil and stir well.

Put the oil in a large ovenproof frying pan over a high heat. Rinse the snapper fillets in cold water and pat them dry with paper towel. Season the fillets liberally with sea salt and put them skin side down in the hot pan. Sear the fillets for a minute or two until the skin is crisply golden and then turn them over.

Put the pan into the oven and bake the snapper for 8 minutes, then transfer the fillets to a serving dish. Spoon the citrus dressing over and serve immediately.

tuna salad with
fried lemon zest   serves 4

4 x 200 g (7 oz) tuna steaks
5 tablespoons olive oil
1 tablespoon lemon juice
1 tablespoon lemon thyme leaves
2 handfuls baby rocket (arugula) leaves
2 handfuls radicchio leaves
2 handfuls mizuna leaves
250 g (9 oz) cherry tomatoes
90 g (3 1/4 oz/ 1/2 cup) small black olives
1 telegraph (long) cucumber, peeled
  and seeded
2 lemons
1 handful flat-leaf (Italian) parsley
extra virgin olive oil, to serve
lemon wedges, to serve

Cut the tuna steaks into several large pieces and cover with 3 tablespoons of the olive oil, lemon juice and thyme. Allow to marinate for several hours. Put the salad leaves, cherry tomatoes and olives onto a serving platter. Cut the cucumber into large bite-sized chunks and add to the salad.

Remove the zest from 2 lemons with a vegetable peeler and cut into thin strips. Heat the remaining olive oil in a small frying pan over a medium heat. Cook the zest for 3 minutes and remove as it begins to turn golden brown. Drain on paper towel.

Heat a non-stick frying pan or grill (broiler) and sear the tuna for a minute on all sides. Arrange the tuna pieces over the salad and scatter with the fried lemon zest and parsley leaves. Drizzle with a little extra virgin olive oil and serve with wedges of fresh lemon.

hokkien noodle stir-fry

serves 4

550 g (1 lb 4 oz/1 bunch) bok choy
   (pak choi)
1 telegraph (long) cucumber
1 tablespoon peanut oil
2 garlic cloves, finely chopped
2 large red chillies, seeded and finely
   sliced
1 tablespoon grated fresh ginger
1 red onion, sliced
1 red capsicum (pepper), finely sliced
450 g (1 lb) fresh hokkien (egg) noodles
3 tablespoons kecap manis
1 tablespoon black sesame seeds,
   to serve

Rinse the bok choy and slice it into halves or quarters depending on its size. Peel the telegraph cucumber, slice it in half lengthways and, using a teaspoon, remove the seeds, then cut the cucumber into thick slices on the diagonal.

Heat the peanut oil in a wok over medium heat and add the garlic, chillies, ginger and onion. Stir-fry until the onion is soft, then remove and set aside. Add the bok choy, cucumber and capsicum to the wok and stir-fry until the bok choy is soft and wilted. Remove and set aside. Add the noodles and kecap manis and stir-fry until the noodles are heated through. Return the vegetables to the wok and stir-fry for 1 minute. Divide among four plates and sprinkle with the black sesame seeds, to serve.

lemon thyme roast chicken

serves 4

1.8 kg (4 lb) whole chicken
1 bunch lemon thyme
3 lemons
1 onion, quartered
40 g (1½ oz) butter, softened

Preheat the oven to 200°C (400°F/ Gas 6). Rinse the chicken and pat it dry with paper towel. Scatter some of the lemon thyme over the base of a roasting tin, then generously rub the chicken skin with salt and put it on top of the lemon thyme, breast side up.

Halve one of the lemons and put it inside the chicken, along with the onion quarters and some lemon thyme. Rub the softened butter over the breast and put the chicken in the oven for 1 hour and 15 minutes or until it is cooked through. Take the chicken out and check that it is cooked by pulling a leg away from the body — the juices that run out should be clear and not pink.

Squeeze the two remaining lemons over the chicken and put it back in the oven for a further 5 minutes. Remove the chicken from the oven and allow it to rest for 10 minutes before carving. Arrange the chicken pieces on a serving platter and pour some of the lemony pan juices over them.

pan-fried fish with lemon and black bean sauce

serves 4

1 tablespoon olive oil

2 spring onions (scallions), trimmed and finely sliced

1 red capsicum (pepper), finely diced

2 tablespoons salted black beans, rinsed and drained

250 ml (9 fl oz/1 cup) fish stock (basics)

1 lemon, juiced

1 tablespoon plain (all-purpose) flour

1/2 teaspoon sea salt

4 x 160 g (5 3/4 oz) firm white fish fillets

125 ml (4 fl oz/ 1/2 cup) peanut oil

To make the lemon and black bean sauce, heat the olive oil in a frying pan over a medium heat and add the spring onions and capsicum. Cook for 5 minutes, or until the capsicum is soft. Add the black beans and stock and cook until reduced by half. Add the lemon juice then pour into a small bowl. Wipe out the pan with paper towel to clean.

Put the flour into a plastic bag with the sea salt and freshly ground black pepper. Add the fish fillets and toss until they are lightly coated with flour. Heat the peanut oil in the frying pan over a high heat. Add the fish and cook for 2 minutes, turn the fish over and reduce the heat to medium. Cook for a further 5 minutes. Put the fish onto a serving plate and spoon over the sauce. Serve with steamed greens and rice.

lemon pasta

3 tablespoons extra virgin olive oil
15 basil leaves, finely sliced
3 tablespoons roughly chopped
  flat-leaf (Italian) parsley
2 garlic cloves, minced
2 lemons, zested and juiced
500 g (1 lb 2 oz) casareccia pasta
75 g (2^1/$_2$ oz/^{3}/$_4$ cup) finely grated
  parmesan cheese

Bring a large pot of salted water to the boil. Put the olive oil, basil, parsley, garlic, lemon zest and juice into a bowl and stir to combine. Put the casareccia in a pot of boiling water and cook until *al dente*. Drain the pasta and return it to the warm pot. Add the lemon and herb oil and stir the pasta until it is well coated. Then add the parmesan cheese and stir again. Season with sea salt and freshly ground black pepper.

seared lime salmon with poppy seeds

serves 4

4 x 175 g (6 oz) salmon fillets, skin on
3 limes
1 tablespoon soy sauce
3 tablespoons olive oil
3 tablespoons mirin
1 tablespoon poppy seeds, to serve
steamed rice, to serve

Preheat the grill (broiler). Rinse the salmon fillets in cold water and pat them dry with paper towel. Put the salmon in a bowl and add the juice of two of the limes, the soy sauce and the olive oil. Leave to marinate for half an hour. Remove the skin from the remaining lime and slice it into paper-thin circles. Heat a large non-stick frying pan over high heat and sear the salmon, skin side up, for a minute. Turn each of the fillets over and take the pan off the heat.

Top the salmon fillets with the sliced lime and spoon over the mirin. Grill the fish for 3–4 minutes or until the salmon is cooked and the lime has caramelized. Sprinkle with the poppy seeds. Serve with steamed rice.

aromatic noodles
with seared salmon   serves 4

200 g (7 oz) buckwheat (soba) noodles
2 tablespoons olive oil
4 x 180 g (6 oz) salmon fillets
1 teaspoon sesame oil
1 tablespoon finely grated fresh ginger
2 garlic cloves, crushed
2 large red chillies, seeded and finely
   chopped
4 spring onions (scallions), finely sliced
1 teaspoon lime juice
1 tablespoon soy sauce
1 teaspoon fish sauce
30 g (1 oz/1 bunch) garlic chives,
   snipped into 2 cm (3/4 in) lengths

Bring a large pot of water to the boil and cook the noodles until they are *al dente*. Drain and rinse under cold running water and set aside.

Heat a large frying pan or wok over a high heat and add half the olive oil. When the oil is hot, add the salmon, skin side down, and cook for 1 minute. Turn and cook for another 2 minutes before removing from the pan.

Drain the oil and return the pan to the heat. Add the sesame oil and the rest of the olive oil. Add the ginger, garlic, chillies, spring onions, lime juice, soy and fish sauces. Stir-fry for 1 minute. Add the noodles, tossing until they are coated. Remove from the heat. Add the chives. Toss again. Divide the noodles between four bowls and top with the salmon.

steamed fish
with fresh ginger

serves 4

4 x 125 g (4¹/2 oz) perch or firm white
fish fillets
3 spring onions (scallions), finely sliced
diagonally
4 cm (1¹/2 in) piece young ginger, finely
julienned
80 ml (2¹/2 fl oz/¹/3 cup) peanut oil
lemon wedges, to serve
steamed white rice, to serve

Bring a large pot of water to the boil
then put a steamer basket on top.
Steam the fish for 5 minutes, or until it
is cooked through. Meanwhile, put the
spring onions and ginger in a metal
bowl. Heat the peanut oil in a frying
pan until it begins to smoke. Carefully
pour the very hot oil over the ginger
and spring onions and allow the oil to
absorb the flavours.

Put the fish on warm serving plates
and spoon over the ginger oil. Serve
with lemon wedges and steamed
white rice.

lemon and saffron risotto

serves 4

1 litre (35 fl oz/4 cups) vegetable stock
(basics)
50 g (1³/4 oz) butter
1 onion, finely diced
15 saffron threads
275 g (9³/4 oz/1¹/4 cups) arborio
(risotto) rice
155 g (5¹/2 oz/1 bunch) asparagus
2 tablespoons lemon juice
80 g (2²/3 oz/³/4 cup) grated parmesan
cheese

Heat the stock in a large saucepan over a high heat. When it is almost boiling, reduce the heat to a simmer. Melt the butter in a large heavy-based saucepan over a medium heat. Add the onion and saffron and cook until the onion is soft and transparent. Add the rice and stir until the grains are glossy and well coated in the buttery saffron. Add 250 ml (9 fl oz/ 1 cup) of hot stock and stir until it is absorbed. Continue to add the stock until it is all absorbed and the rice is tender.

Bring a saucepan of water to the boil and quickly blanch the asparagus until it is bright green. Drain and slice into small pieces. Add the lemon juice and parmesan cheese to the risotto and season with sea salt and freshly ground black pepper. Spoon the risotto into warm bowls and top with the asparagus spears.

wild mushroom spaghetti

serves 4

10 g (1/4 oz) dried porcini mushrooms
3 tablespoons olive oil
2 garlic cloves, chopped
1 onion, finely diced
2 field mushrooms, finely sliced
100 g (3 1/2 oz) shiitake mushrooms,
  sliced
1/2 teaspoon thyme leaves
125 ml (4 fl oz/1/2 cup) white wine
100 g (3 1/2 oz) enoki mushrooms
400 g (14 oz) spaghetti
75 g (2 1/2 oz/3/4 cup) finely grated
  parmesan cheese

Bring a large saucepan of water to the boil for the pasta. Soak the dried mushrooms in 250 ml (9 fl oz/1 cup) of boiling water for 15 minutes.

Heat the olive oil and fry the garlic and onions over a medium heat until they are soft and golden. Drain the mushrooms, straining the soaking liquid into a jug. Roughly slice the soaked mushrooms and add them to the onions, together with the field mushrooms, shiitake mushrooms and thyme. Cook them until the field mushrooms are soft and then add the white wine, mushroom soaking liquid and the enoki mushrooms. Season and reduce the heat to a low simmer. Cook the pasta until *al dente*, then drain and return it to the warm pot. Add the parmesan cheese and stir through before dividing the pasta between four bowls. Top with the wild mushroom sauce.

seared snapper with lime salsa

2 teaspoons fish sauce

2 tablespoons lime juice

4 tablespoons olive oil

1/2 teaspoon palm sugar (jaggery) or
   soft brown sugar

1 ripe avocado, flesh diced

1 lime, segments finely diced

1 Lebanese (short) cucumber

1/2 red onion, finely diced

2 large red chillies, seeded and very
   finely sliced

1 handful coriander (cilantro) leaves

4 x 200 g (7 oz) snapper or firm white
   fish fillets, skin on

Put the fish sauce, lime juice, olive oil and sugar into a bowl and stir until the sugar has dissolved. Add the diced avocado, lime, cucumber, red onion, chilli and coriander leaves and toss together. Season to taste with sea salt and freshly ground black pepper.

Rinse the fish fillets and pat them dry with paper towel. Put the vegetable oil into a large ovenproof frying pan over high heat. Season the fillets with sea salt and put them, skin side down, in the hot pan. Sear the fillets for a minute or two until the skin is crisply golden and turn over.

Put the pan in the oven and bake the fish for 8 minutes. Transfer to a serving dish and spoon over the salsa. Serve with boiled new potatoes.

pan-fried whiting with green bean, watercress and fennel salad
serves 4

60 ml (2 fl oz/1/4 cup) lemon juice
125 ml (4 fl oz/1/2 cup) olive oil
2 tablespoons finely chopped mint
2 tablespoons finely chopped dill
1 garlic clove, crushed
12 small whiting or delicate white
  fish fillets
2 handfuls picked watercress
100 g (31/2 oz/3/4 cup) blanched green
  beans
1 fennel bulb, finely sliced

Put the lemon juice, olive oil, mint, dill and garlic into a large bowl and mix well. Rinse the fish fillets in cold water and pat dry with paper towel. Toss the fillets in the marinade, cover and leave to marinate for a few hours in the fridge. Heat a large non-stick frying pan over a high heat. Cook the whiting for 1–2 minutes on each side, then take the fillets out of the pan. Add any remaining marinade to the pan and cook for a minute.

Toss the watercress, beans and fennel together and pile on 4 plates. Top with the fish and a light drizzle of the marinade sauce.

chinese omelette   serves 4

3 eggs
1 tablespoon mirin
1/2 teaspoon soy sauce
250 g (9 oz) fresh crab meat, shredded
1 teaspoon lemon juice
1 teaspoon olive oil
90 g (3¹/4oz/1 cup) bean sprouts,
   trimmed
20 g (³/4 oz/¹/2 cup) water spinach tips
2 teaspoons vegetable oil
2 shallots, finely sliced on the diagonal
1 large red chilli, finely sliced

Whisk together the eggs, mirin and soy sauce. Season with a little pepper and sea salt and set to one side. In a bowl, combine the crab meat, lemon juice and olive oil. Season with a little sea salt and freshly ground black pepper and toss to combine. Add the sprouts and water spinach tips and set to one side.

Heat a small non-stick frying pan over a medium heat and add 1/2 teaspoon of vegetable oil. Ladle in some of the egg mix and swirl around so that the egg finely coats the base of the pan. Continue to cook until the egg has cooked through then remove by sliding the omelette onto a plate. Repeat with the remaining mixture adding oil to the pan as it is needed, till you have 4 thin omelettes. Put each omelette onto a warm serving plate, add the crab mix and roll half the omelette over the filling. Sprinkle with the shallots and chilli to serve.

penne with rocket, chilli
and parmesan cheese   serves 4

400 g (14 oz) penne pasta
1 chilli, seeded and finely chopped
1 tablespoon salted capers
4 tablespoons extra virgin olive oil
1 bunch rocket (arugula), rinsed and
   roughly chopped
100 g (3½ oz/1 cup) parmesan cheese,
   grated

Bring a large pot of salted water to the boil and cook the pasta till *al dente*. Drain the pasta and then return it to the warm pot. Add the chilli, capers, olive oil, rocket and half the parmesan cheese.

Toss together all the ingredients until the rocket is lightly wilted, then spoon the pasta into 4 warm pasta plates. Sprinkle with the remaining parmesan cheese and serve.

deep-fried whitebait serves 4

500 g (1 lb 2 oz) whitebait
1 teaspoon sea salt
750 ml (26 fl oz/3 cups) sunflower oil
125 g (4¹/₂ oz/1 cup) plain
  (all-purpose) flour
¹/₂ teaspoon paprika
fresh bread, buttered, to serve

Rinse the whitebait under running cold water then drain in a colander or large sieve. Put the flour, paprika and the sea salt into a large bowl and stir to mix well.

Heat the oil in a large deep saucepan until the surface begins to shimmer and a pinch of flour dropped into the oil fries immediately.

Add the whitebait to the seasoned flour, tossing until all the fish are well coated. With your fingers, lift the whitebait away from the bowl and shake free of any excess flour. Deep-fry the whitebait in batches for about 3 minutes or until crisp and golden. Serve with a sprinkle of sea salt, lemon wedges and slices of buttered fresh bread.

chargrilled capsicum with boiled egg and anchovy serves 4

4 red capsicums (peppers)
4 eggs, at room temperature
3 tablespoons extra virgin olive oil
8 radicchio leaves
8 anchovy fillets
1 tablespoon salted capers

Chargrill or roast the red capsicums until their skins are blackened. Place them into a bowl and cover with plastic wrap until they have cooled. Bring a pot of water to the boil and then add the eggs. Boil the eggs for 5 minutes, then remove them from the pan and allow to cool. Rub the blackened skin from the capsicums and then cut or tear the flesh into long strips.

Put the strips into a bowl and add the olive oil and some sea salt and freshly ground black pepper. Toss to coat the capsicum strips. Peel the eggs. Tear the radicchio leaves in half and divide them between 4 plates. Top with the marinated capsicum, anchovies and capers. Cut the eggs in half and add them to the salad. Drizzle with any of the remaining capsicum oil and serve.

blue-eye cod with lime pickle sauce

2 large handfuls flat-leaf (Italian)
  parsley leaves
4 anchovies
1 teaspoon small capers
10 mint leaves
1 tablespoon Indian lime pickle
80 ml (2½ fl oz/⅓ cup) light olive oil
2 tablespoons olive oil
4 x 150 g (5½ oz) blue-eye cod or
  firm white fish fillets
boiled new potatoes, to serve

Put the parsley, anchovies, capers, mint, lime pickle and light olive oil into a food processor or blender and blend to form a thick sauce. Set aside.

Rinse the fish fillets under running water then pat them dry with paper towel. Heat the oil in a non-stick frying pan over a high heat and add the fillets. Cook for 2 minutes then turn them over. Reduce the heat to medium and cook for a further 3–4 minutes depending on how thick the fillets are.

Serve the fish with a spoonful of the sauce and boiled new potatoes.

fresh egg noodle salad

serves 4

200 g (7 oz) fresh egg noodles
75 g (2³/₄ oz/1 cup) finely sliced
  Chinese cabbage
2 spring onions (scallions), finely sliced
100 g (3¹/₂ oz/1 cup) bean sprouts
1 carrot, peeled and grated
1 red capsicum (pepper), julienned
2 handfuls coriander (cilantro) leaves
3 tablespoons hoisin sauce
1¹/₂ tablespoons lime juice
1 teaspoon sesame oil
1 teaspoon sugar
2 tablespoons sesame seeds

Bring a large pot of salted water to the boil and add the fresh egg noodles. Cook until *al dente* then remove and drain. Rinse under running cold water and set to one side. Into a large bowl put the Chinese cabbage, spring onions, bean sprouts, carrot, red capsicum and coriander.

In a small bowl combine the hoisin sauce, lime juice, sesame oil and sugar. Stir to combine then pour over the vegetables. Rinse the noodles one more time under cold water then drain and roughly cut the noodles with a pair of kitchen scissors. Add to the other ingredients. Toss several times so that all the noodles and vegetables are coated in the dressing. Pile the noodles into a large serving bowl. Toast the sesame seeds in a pan over a medium heat until golden brown then sprinkle over the salad.

citrus compote breakfast trifles honey-toasted fruit muesli coconut bread banana pancakes with pineapple syrup banana bread pineapple muffins quick fix baked passionfruit soufflé vanilla-poached apricots nectarine and almond cake lemon ricotta cake nectarine and hazelnut torte passionfruit melting moments white peach ice cream almond and pine nut cake vanilla panna cotta with toffee apples vanilla

04 sweets

poached white peaches with mint passionfruit curd with pistachio biscotti anzac biscuits chestnut cakes with lemon icing marinated plums with toasted madeira cake citrus syrup cake creamed rice with vanilla-glazed oranges pineapple fruit salad lemon

citrus compote

makes 8-10 small serves or 4 regular serves

3 limes
3 oranges
2 pink grapefruits
1 vanilla bean, finely chopped
1 teaspoon sugar
250 g (9 oz/1 cup) honey-flavoured
  yoghurt

Zest 1 lime and 1 orange and put in a bowl. Peel the limes, oranges and grapefruits with a sharp knife. Cut the flesh into segments, or thinly slice, saving any juice. Add the vanilla bean, sugar and reserved juice and mix to combine. Serve with honey yoghurt.

breakfast trifles

makes 8 small glasses

375 g (13 oz/1¹/2 cups) honey-flavoured
  yoghurt
200 g (7 oz/2 cups) toasted muesli
440 g (15¹/2 oz) fruit of choice, such as
  diced mangoes, peaches or mixed
  berries

Stir the yoghurt well until it is smooth and creamy. Layer the muesli, yoghurt and fruit into small glasses, finishing with fruit on top. Serve accompanied with a small spoon.

honey-toasted fruit muesli

makes 12 serves

500 g (1 lb 2 oz/5 cups) rolled
(porridge) oats
125 g (4¹/₂ oz/1 cup) unsalted
sunflower seeds
125 g (4¹/₂ oz/1 cup) slivered almonds
100 g (3¹/₂ oz/1 cup) triticale
60 g (2¹/₄ oz/1 cup) shredded coconut
2 tablespoons sesame seeds
250 g (9 oz/³/₄ cup) honey
4 tablespoons vegetable oil
50 g (1³/₄ oz/¹/₄ cup) dried apricots,
finely sliced
25 g (1 oz/¹/₃ cup) dried apples, finely
sliced
50 g (1³/₄ oz/²/₃ cup) dried peaches,
finely sliced

Preheat the oven to 150°C (300°F/ Gas 2). Put the rolled oats into a large bowl. Add the sunflower seeds, slivered almonds, triticale, shredded coconut and sesame seeds. Stir to combine. Heat the honey and the vegetable oil in a saucepan over low heat. Pour the warm honey mixture over the dry ingredients and stir until they are well coated. Spread the mixture on a baking tray and bake for 30 minutes, stirring occasionally. Remove from the oven and allow to cool. Add the dried apricots, apples and peaches. Toss to combine. Store the muesli in an airtight container.

coconut bread

2 eggs
300 ml (10^1/$_2$ fl oz/1^1/$_4$ cups) milk
70 g (2^1/$_2$ oz) unsalted butter
300 g (10^1/$_2$ oz/2^1/$_2$ cups) plain
  (all-purpose) flour
2 teaspoons baking powder
2 teaspoons ground cinnamon
225 g (8 oz/1 cup) caster (superfine)
  sugar
150 g (5^1/$_2$ oz/2^1/$_2$ cups) shredded
  coconut
banana, sliced, to serve

Preheat the oven to 180°C (350°F/ Gas 4). Put the eggs and milk into a bowl and lightly whisk. Melt the butter and set aside. Sift the plain flour, baking powder and cinnamon into a mixing bowl. Add the caster sugar and coconut. Make a well in the centre and gradually stir in the milk mixture until combined. Add the melted butter and stir until the mixture is just smooth.

Pour the mixture into a greased and lined 21 x 10 cm (8^1/$_4$ x 4 in) loaf (bar) tin and bake for 1 hour, or until a skewer inserted into the centre comes out clean. Allow to cool before removing from the loaf tin. Serve in buttery toasted slices with or without sliced banana.

banana pancakes with pineapple syrup

pancake mixture

125 g (4¹/2 oz/1 cup) self-raising flour
40 g (1¹/2 oz/¹/4cup) caster (superfine) sugar
1 egg
150 ml (5 fl oz) milk

95 g (3¹/4 oz/¹/2 cup) grated palm sugar (jaggery) or soft brown sugar
250 ml (9 fl oz/1 cup) fresh pineapple juice
1 tablespoon lime juice
2 bananas
2 tablespoons caster (superfine) sugar
30 g (1 oz) unsalted butter

To make the pancakes, put the flour, sugar and ¹/2 teaspoon of salt in a bowl. In a separate bowl, beat the egg and milk together. Pour into the flour mixture and lightly fold together. Allow the batter to rest for 10 minutes before using.

To make the syrup, put the sugar and pineapple juice in a small saucepan over high heat and bring to the boil. Reduce the heat and simmer until the juice has reduced by half and formed a syrup. Remove from the heat and stir through the lime juice.

Slice the banana thinly and toss the slices in caster sugar. Heat a little butter in a frying pan over medium heat. Add a tablespoon of the pancake mixture to the pan and allow to cook for 1 minute. Top with banana and cook until bubbles appear. Turn and cook the pancake for a further 2 minutes. Remove and keep in a warm place. Repeat with the remaining batter and banana, adding more butter to the pan as required. Serve with a drizzle of the pineapple syrup.

banana bread

makes 1 loaf

90 g (3¹/₄ oz) butter, softened
115 g (4 oz/¹/₂ cup) caster (superfine)
  sugar
2 eggs
1 teaspoon natural vanilla extract
250 g (9 oz/2 cups) plain (all-purpose)
  flour
2 teaspoons baking powder
2 large ripe bananas
1 orange, zested
honey or maple syrup, to serve

Preheat the oven to 180°C (350°F/ Gas 4). Put the butter, caster sugar, eggs, vanilla extract, flour, baking powder, bananas and orange zest into a food processor. Process to a smooth batter. Spoon into a greased and lined 8 x 16 cm (3¹/₄ x 6¹/₄ in) loaf (bar) tin. Bake for 1 hour, or until a skewer inserted into the centre comes out clean. Serve in warm slices or toasted with butter and a drizzle of honey or maple syrup.

pineapple muffins   makes 18

215 g (7¹/2 oz/1³/4 cups) plain
  (all-purpose) flour
2 teaspoons baking powder
165 g (5³/4 oz/³/4 cup) sugar
¹/2 teaspoon ground cinnamon
115 g (4 oz/1¹/4 cups) desiccated
  coconut
45 g (1¹/2 oz) unsalted butter, melted
185 ml (6 fl oz/³/4 cup) milk
2 eggs
190 g (6³/4 oz/1 cup) diced fresh
  pineapple

Preheat the oven to 180°C (350°F/
Gas 4). Sift the flour, baking powder
and a pinch of salt into a large mixing
bowl. Add the sugar, cinnamon and
coconut and stir to combine. Make a
well in the centre of the mixture and
add the melted butter, milk and eggs.
Mix until just combined and then fold
the pineapple through.

Grease two small muffin trays (lined
with paper cases if desired) and put a
heaped tablespoon of the mixture into
each hole. Bake for 15–17 minutes, or
until golden brown.

quick fix

makes 18

4 puff pastry sheets
icing sugar, to sprinkle
fresh berries, to serve
whipped cream flavoured with natural
vanilla extract, to serve

Preheat the oven to 180ºC (350ºF/ Gas 4). Cut the puff pastry sheets into 3 x 8 cm (1¼ x 3 in) strips. Put them on a greased tray lined with baking paper, and bake in the oven for 15 minutes, or until golden brown. Remove from the oven, sprinkle with icing sugar and serve with fresh berries and the vanilla-flavoured whipped cream.

baked passionfruit soufflé

serves 6

7 eggs, separated
115 g (4 oz/1/2 cup) sugar
4 tablespoons passionfruit pulp
1 teaspoon cornflour (cornstarch)
caster (superfine) sugar, to serve

Preheat the oven to 200°C (400°F/ Gas 6). Grease six 300 ml (10 1/2 fl oz) ramekins. Sprinkle the ramekin bases with sugar to coat before tipping out excess sugar. Put 5 egg yolks (discard 2 yolks) into a metal bowl with the sugar and whisk until very thick and pale yellow.

Put the bowl over a saucepan of simmering water and stir gently until the mixture thickens and is hot to touch. Remove from the heat and put the bowl into a sink filled with iced water. Stir until cool. Fold in the passionfruit pulp. In a separate bowl, beat the egg whites until soft peaks form. Add the cornflour and beat for 1 minute. Fold half the beaten egg whites through the passionfruit mixture until well blended and then lightly fold in the remaining egg whites.

Spoon the batter into the ramekins, filling to within 1 cm (1/2 in) of the top. Bake for 5 minutes, then reduce the temperature to 180°C (350°F/Gas 4) and bake for 12 minutes, or until the soufflés have risen and the tops are golden brown. Remove from the oven and sprinkle with icing sugar to serve.

vanilla-poached apricots

serves 6

200 g (7 oz/1 cup) dried apricots
1 vanilla bean, halved lengthways
1/2 teaspoon rosewater
1 tablespoon honey
40 g (1 1/2 oz/ 1/3 cup) toasted slivered
  almonds
250 g (9 oz/1 cup) plain yoghurt or
  warm custard

Put the apricots in a saucepan with
the split vanilla bean and 625 ml
(21 1/2 fl oz/2 1/2 cups) of water. Bring to
the boil, then cover and allow the fruit
to simmer on a low heat for an hour.
Remove the vanilla bean and stir in the
rosewater and the honey. Serve with
the toasted almonds and yoghurt, or a
swirl of warm custard.

nectarine and almond cake

3 eggs
125 ml (4 fl oz/1/2 cup) milk
300 g (101/2 oz/11/3 cups) caster
  (superfine) sugar
250 g (9 oz/2 cups) plain (all-purpose)
  flour
2 teaspoons baking powder
1 teaspoon natural vanilla extract
8 nectarines, stones removed
55 g (2 oz/1/2 cup) ground almonds
40 g (11/2 oz) unsalted butter

Preheat the oven to 180°C (350°F/ Gas 4). Grease and line a 23 cm (9 in) spring-form cake tin. Combine the eggs, milk, sugar, flour, baking powder and vanilla extract in a food processor and process to form a thick batter. Scrape the batter into a bowl. Slice the nectarines into eighths and fold the fruit pieces through the batter.

Spoon the batter into the prepared tin and top with the ground almonds and dobs of the butter. Bake for 40 minutes. Test with a skewer to ensure that the cake is cooked through, then remove the tin from the oven and allow the cake to cool before serving.

lemon ricotta cake   serves 10

125 g (4¹/2 oz/1 cup) sultanas (golden
  raisins)
250 ml (9 fl oz/1 cup) very strong Earl
  Grey tea
6 eggs, separated
500 g (1 lb 2 oz/2 cups) firm ricotta
  cheese
125 ml (4 fl oz/¹/2 cup) thick
  (heavy/double) cream
125 g (4¹/2 oz/¹/2 cup) caster (superfine)
  sugar
3 lemons, zested
lemon and Cointreau syrup (basics)
vanilla ice cream (page 282), to serve

Preheat the oven to 180°C (350°F/
Gas 4). Line a 20 cm (8 in) spring-form
cake tin with baking paper.

Put the sultanas into the Earl Grey tea
and allow them to soak. Whip the egg
whites until they form stiff peaks. Put
the ricotta cheese, egg yolks, cream,
sugar and lemon zest into a large
bowl and blend everything together.
Drain the sultanas and add them to
the ricotta mix before carefully folding
in the egg whites.

Pour the mixture into the cake tin and
bake for 40 minutes, then put a layer
of foil over the cake to stop it burning
and bake for a further 15 minutes.
Test that the cake is firm — a skewer
should come out clean when inserted
into the centre of the cake. Allow to
cool in the tin, before turning out.
Serve with lemon and Cointreau syrup
and vanilla ice cream.

nectarine and hazelnut torte

serves 6

115 g (4 oz/^{1}/$_2$ cup) caster (superfine) sugar

1 cinnamon stick

1 vanilla bean, halved lengthways

9 nectarines, quartered and stones removed

4 eggs

80 g (2^3/$_4$ oz/^{2}/$_3$ cup) icing (confectioners') sugar

50 g (1^3/$_4$ oz/^{1}/$_2$ cup) plain (all-purpose) flour

3 tablespoons hazelnut meal

30 g (1 oz) butter, melted

whipped cream, to serve

Preheat the oven to 180°C (350°F/ Gas 4). Put the sugar, cinnamon and vanilla bean into a small saucepan and add 250 ml (9 fl oz/1 cup) of water. Bring to the boil then reduce the heat and simmer for 5 minutes. Add the nectarines and cook for 3 minutes. Remove with a slotted spoon and set aside in a bowl. Reduce the syrup by half then pour it over the nectarines. Allow to cool.

Put the eggs and icing sugar in a heatproof bowl set over a saucepan of boiling water, making sure the base does not touch the water. Beat until the mixture is just warm then remove from the heat. Continue to beat until it triples in volume. Fold in the flour, hazelnut meal and butter. Spoon into a lined shallow 24 x 34 cm (9^1/$_2$ x 13^1/$_2$ in) cake tin. Bake for 20 minutes. Turn out onto a flat surface, cut into large squares and put on dessert plates. Spoon the nectarines over the cake. Top with whipped cream and drizzle with the syrup.

passionfruit melting moments

makes 36

125 g (4¹/2 oz) unsalted butter, chilled
  and cubed
30 g (1 oz/¹/4 cup) icing (confectioners')
  sugar
90 g (3¹/4 oz/³/4 cup) plain (all-purpose)
  flour
30 g (1 oz/¹/4 cup) cornflour
  (cornstarch)
1 tablespoon passionfruit pulp

lime butter
60 g (2¹/4 oz) unsalted butter, softened
125 g (4¹/2 oz/1 cup) icing
  (confectioners') sugar
1 teaspoon grated lime zest
2 teaspoons lime juice
icing (confectioners') sugar, extra,
  to dust

Preheat the oven to 160°C (315°F/ Gas 2–3). Put the butter, icing sugar, flour and cornflour in a food processor and process in short bursts until the mixture just comes together. Fold through the passionfruit pulp. Pipe the mixture in 1 teaspoon amounts onto a baking tray lined with baking paper. Bake for 15–20 minutes, or until the biscuits are just lightly golden brown. Remove and cool on a wire rack.

To make the lime butter, put the butter, icing sugar and lime zest in a mixing bowl and beat until the mixture is white. Fold through the lime juice.

Join two biscuits together with lime butter and lightly dust with icing sugar. Repeat with other biscuits.

white peach ice cream

serves 6

3 large white peaches, stoned and
  peeled
3 tablespoons Cointreau
2 tablespoons lemon juice
1 teaspoon rosewater
4–6 tablespoons caster (superfine)
  sugar
315 ml (10³/4 fl oz/1¹/4 cups) cream
  (whipping), whipped
45 g (1¹/2 oz/¹/2 cup) toasted almond
  flakes

Cut the peaches into small cubes and mix them with the liqueur, lemon juice, rosewater and caster sugar, stirring until the sugar dissolves.

Fold the fruit into the whipped cream, then stir in the almonds to combine. Pour the mixture into a 22 x 8 x 7 cm (8¹/2 x 3¹/4 x 2³/4 in) loaf (bar) tin or mould and freeze it overnight.

Unmould the ice cream by dipping it briefly into hot water before turning it out. Serve the ice cream in slices on chilled plates.

almond and pine nut cake

serves 8

40 g (1¹/2 oz) unsalted butter
2 mandarins
250 g (9 oz/1²/3 cups) raw almonds
300 g (10¹/2 oz/1¹/3 cups) caster
  (superfine) sugar
¹/2 teaspoon ground cinnamon
8 egg whites
85 g (3 oz/²/3 cup) plain (all-purpose)
  flour, sifted
4 tablespoons pine nuts
3 tablespoons dessert wine or Grand
  Marnier
icing (confectioners') sugar, to dust
mandarin salad (basics), to serve
whipped cream, to serve

Preheat the oven to 180°C (350°F/ Gas 4). Grease a 20 cm (8 in) springform cake tin with the butter. Peel mandarins and, with a sharp knife, finely chop the zest. Put 3 tablespoons of zest into a food processor. Add the almonds, sugar and cinnamon and process to a fine consistency.

Beat the egg whites with a pinch of salt until stiff peaks form. Lightly fold the almond mixture into the egg whites then add the flour. Spoon the batter into the prepared tin and sprinkle with the pine nuts. Bake for 1 hour, or until a skewer inserted into the centre of the cake comes out clean. Allow to cool before serving.

Pour the dessert wine or Grand Marnier over the cake then dust with icing sugar. Serve with mandarin salad and cream.

vanilla panna cotta
with toffee apples   serves 8

875 ml (30 fl oz/3$\frac{1}{2}$ cups) cream
   (whipping)
2 lemons, zest finely grated, juiced
115 g (4 oz/$\frac{1}{2}$ cup) caster (superfine)
   sugar
2 vanilla beans, halved lengthways
3 gelatine sheets
toffee apples (basics), to serve

Whip 250 ml (9 fl oz/1 cup) of cream and put it in the fridge. Put the rest of the cream, lemon zest and juice, sugar and vanilla in a saucepan and heat gently over a low heat to melt the sugar. Do not let it boil.

Take the pan off the heat and, using the end of a sharp knife, scrape the seeds from the inside of each of the vanilla pods into the cream mixture (you can keep the pods for later use). Soak the gelatine sheets in a bowl of cold water. When the sheets are soft, squeeze out any excess water and stir them into the warm cream.

Allow the vanilla cream to cool before lightly folding through the whipped cream. Pour the mixture into eight tea cups or moulds, cover with plastic wrap and chill in the fridge for 3 hours or overnight. The panna cottas can be served in their cups, or you can turn them out by dipping the base of each of the moulds into a bowl of hot water and upending them onto the plate. Give them a little shake to loosen them. Serve with warm toffee apples.

vanilla poached white peaches with mint

serves 6

440 g (15¹/2 oz/2 cups) sugar
2 vanilla beans, halved lengthways
6 ripe white peaches, cut in half and
    stones removed
1 tablespoon lemon juice
20 mint leaves, to garnish
vanilla ice cream (see page 282),
    to serve

Put the sugar and vanilla beans into a large saucepan with 1 litre (35 fl oz/ 4 cups) of water. Bring to the boil and simmer for a few minutes. Put the peaches into the syrup, skin side up, and cook for 2 minutes. With a large spoon, carefully turn the peaches over and cook for a further few minutes. Depending on the size of the peaches, you may have to do this in batches. With the point of a sharp knife, test to see if the peaches are cooked. They should still be firm, but give little resistance to the knife. Remove with a slotted spoon and put into a large bowl. Leave the syrup on the heat to reduce for a few minutes.

Carefully peel the peaches then pour over the syrup and set aside to cool. When the syrup has cooled, add the lemon juice and mint leaves. Serve with vanilla ice cream.

passionfruit curd with pistachio biscotti serves 4-6

5 passionfruit
40 g (1 1/2 oz) unsalted butter
40 g (1 1/2 oz) caster (superfine) sugar
1 whole egg
1 egg yolk
2 teaspoons lime juice
80 ml (2 1/2 fl oz/1/3 cup) cream
  (whipping), whipped
pistachio biscotti (basics), to serve

Remove the pulp from 3 of the passionfruit and strain through a fine sieve, stirring to push the passionfruit juice through. Discard the strained pulp. Put the juice in a bowl with the unstrained pulp of the remaining passionfruit. Melt the butter in a small saucepan over a low heat. When the butter has just melted, add the sugar, passionfruit pulp, egg and egg yolk. Whisk over a medium heat until the mixture is thick and just boiling. Remove from the heat, stir through the lime juice and refrigerate when cool. Fold the passionfruit through the whipped cream just before serving with pistachio biscotti.

anzac biscuits

makes 30

125 g (4¹/₂ oz/1 cup) plain (all-purpose) flour
100 g (3¹/₂ oz/1 cup) rolled (porridge) oats
90 g (3¹/₄ oz/1 cup) desiccated coconut
225 g (8 oz/1 cup) sugar
1 pinch of salt
125 g (4¹/₂ oz) unsalted butter
3 tablespoons golden (dark corn) syrup
2 tablespoons boiling water
1 teaspoon bicarbonate of soda (baking soda)

Preheat the oven to 180°C (350°F/ Gas 4). Grease and line a baking tray with baking paper. Sift the plain flour into a large mixing bowl and add the rolled oats, coconut, sugar and a pinch of salt. Put the butter and golden syrup into a saucepan. Stir over low heat until the butter has melted. Put 2 tablespoons boiling water into a cup and dissolve the bicarbonate of soda. Stir the water and soda into the melted butter, which will cause it to bubble up, then pour it over the dry ingredients. Stir to combine.
Drop spoonfuls of the mixture onto the tray, allowing room for the biscuits to spread. Bake for 12–15 minutes, or until dark gold. Remove from the oven and transfer the biscuits to a wire rack to cool. Store in an airtight container.

chestnut cakes
with lemon icing   makes 12

6 eggs
150 g (5¹/₂ oz/²/₃ cup) caster (superfine)
  sugar
400 g (14 oz) tin chestnut purée
175 g (6 oz/1³/₄ cups) ground almonds
1 teaspoon baking powder
1 quantity lemon icing (basics)

Preheat the oven to 180°C (350°F/ Gas 4). Beat the eggs until light and fluffy, then add the sugar and chestnut purée and beat for 1 minute further. Fold in the ground almonds and baking powder.

Spoon the mixture into a greased 12-hole muffin tin (lined with paper cases if desired) and bake in the oven for 20 minutes, or until the cakes are cooked — a skewer should come out clean when inserted into the centre of the cake. Remove the cakes and allow them to cool before icing with lemon icing.

marinated plums with toasted madeira cake serves 4

400 g (14 oz) ripe plums, stones
  removed, finely sliced
2 tablespoons caster (superfine) sugar
1/2 vanilla bean, finely chopped
125 ml (4 fl oz/1/2 cup) dessert wine
4 slices ready-made madeira (pound)
  cake
vanilla ice cream (see page 282),
  to serve

Put the finely sliced plums, sugar, vanilla bean and dessert wine into a bowl. Stir, then cover the bowl with plastic wrap and put it in the fridge for several hours until you are ready to serve.

Take the plums out of the fridge. Grill the slices of madeira cake on both sides until they are lightly browned.

Put the slices of cake on dessert plates, top with the marinated plums, drizzle with the remaining juice and serve with a scoop of vanilla ice cream.

citrus syrup cake   serves 10

250 g (9 oz) unsalted butter, softened
225 g (8 oz/1 cup) caster (superfine)
   sugar
4 eggs, lightly beaten
250 g (9 oz/2 cups) sifted self-raising
   flour
4 oranges
4 lemons
4 limes
225 g (8 oz/1 cup) sugar

Preheat the oven to 180°C (350°F/ Gas 4). Grease and line a 23 cm (9 in) spring-form cake tin. Beat the butter and caster sugar in a mixing bowl until pale and creamy. Stir in the eggs, then fold in the self-raising flour. Spoon the batter into the cake tin and bake for 50 minutes, or until a skewer inserted into the centre of the cake comes out clean.

Meanwhile, make the syrup. Juice and zest the oranges, lemons and limes. Combine the juice with the sugar in a saucepan over medium heat and stir for 20 minutes, or until the sugar dissolves and a clear syrup is formed. Add the zest and simmer for 1 minute, then remove from the heat. Leave the cooked cake in the tin and pierce it all over with a skewer. Pour most of the syrup over the cake, reserving some of the syrup and the zest. When the cake has cooled, transfer it to a serving plate and spoon over the remaining syrup and zest.

creamed rice with vanilla-glazed oranges

serves 6

110 g (3³/4 oz/¹/2 cup) short grain rice
500 ml (17 fl oz/2 cups) milk
1 vanilla pod, halved lengthways
4 strips lemon zest
4 tablespoons sugar
125 ml (4 fl oz/¹/2 cup) cream
  (whipping), whipped
vanilla-glazed oranges (basics)

Preheat the oven to 180°C (350°F/ Gas 4). Rinse the rice in cold water and drain it. Bring the milk to the boil with the vanilla pod, lemon zest and the sugar. Add the rice and simmer gently for 30 minutes, stirring occasionally. When the rice has cooked, allow it to cool a little and then fold in the whipped cream. Spoon the creamed rice into bowls and serve with the vanilla-glazed oranges.

pineapple fruit salad serves 4

1 pineapple
10 mint leaves
2 teaspoons finely grated fresh ginger
1 teaspoon orange flower water
vanilla ice cream (see page 282) or
   honeyed yoghurt, to serve

Skin the pineapple, cutting out any brown 'eyes'. Cut it into thin slices lengthways, trimming off any bits of woody core, and put the slices in a bowl along with the mint, ginger and orange flower water. Toss to combine, cover and allow to chill for an hour in the fridge. Serve with vanilla ice cream or honeyed yoghurt.

lemon delicious

serves 8

2 lemons

3 eggs

70 g (2^1/$_2$ oz) unsalted butter

175 g (6 oz/^{3}/$_4$ cup) caster (superfine) sugar

3 tablespoons sifted plain (all-purpose) flour

185 ml (6 fl oz/^{3}/$_4$ cup) milk

Preheat the oven to 180°C (350°F/ Gas 4). Grease a large ovenproof dish. Finely grate the zest of the lemons, then juice them. Separate the eggs. In a bowl, beat the butter with the caster sugar and the grated lemon zest until pale and creamy. Add the egg yolks and whisk to combine. Whisk in the plain flour and milk, adding them alternately to make a smooth batter. Add the lemon juice and stir to ensure it is well combined. In a separate bowl, whisk the egg whites until they form stiff peaks and then lightly fold them through the batter. Pour the mixture into the prepared dish and put the dish into a large roasting tin. Fill the tray with enough hot water to reach halfway up the side of the dish. Bake for 1 hour.

vanilla ice cream   serves 4

375 ml (13 fl oz/1¹/2 cups) milk
250 ml (9 fl oz/1 cup) cream (whipping)
2 vanilla beans
5 egg yolks
125 g (4¹/2 oz/heaped ¹/2 cup) caster
   (superfine) sugar

Put the milk and cream into a heavy-based saucepan. Lightly rub the vanilla beans between your fingers to soften them. Cut the pods in half lengthways and put them in the saucepan. Put the saucepan over medium heat and bring the milk and cream just to simmering point. Remove from the heat.

Whisk the egg yolks with the caster sugar in a bowl until light and foamy. Whisk in a little of the warm milk and cream. Add the remaining liquid, reserving the vanilla beans, and whisk to combine. Return the mixture to the cleaned saucepan. Cook over medium heat, stirring constantly with a wooden spoon, until the mixture thickens and coats the back of the spoon. Strain into a bowl. Scrape the vanilla seeds from the split pods into the mixture and stir through.

Allow to cool before churning in an ice cream machine according to the manufacturer's instructions.

lemon slice

125 g (4^1/$_2$ oz) softened unsalted butter
60 g (2^1/$_4$ oz/^{1}/$_2$ cup) icing
(confectioners') sugar, sifted
1 teaspoon natural vanilla extract
175 g (6 oz/scant 1^1/$_2$ cups) self-raising
flour, sifted
1 teaspoon grated lemon zest
90 g (3^1/$_4$ oz/^{3}/$_4$ cup) plain (all-purpose)
flour
^{1}/$_2$ teaspoon baking powder
85 g (3 oz/^{3}/$_4$ cup) ground almonds
3 eggs
225 g (8 oz/1 cup) caster (superfine)
sugar
185 ml (6 fl oz/^{3}/$_4$ cup) lemon juice
2 tablespoons grated lemon zest, extra
icing (confectioners') sugar, to dust

Preheat the oven to 180°C (350°F/ Gas 4). Grease and line a 16 x 26 cm (6^1/$_4$ x 10^1/$_2$ in) slice tin. Beat the butter and the icing sugar in a mixing bowl until pale and creamy. Add the vanilla extract. Stir in the self-raising flour and lemon zest. Press the mixture into the prepared tin. Bake for 15 minutes, or until golden.

Meanwhile, sift the plain flour and baking powder into a bowl. Add the ground almonds. In a separate bowl, beat together the eggs, caster sugar, lemon juice and lemon zest. Stir the egg mixture into the dry ingredients and pour over the already cooked base. Bake for 20 minutes, or until firm. Cool in the tin. Cut into pieces and dust with icing sugar.

mini mandarin cakes makes 16

3 mandarins
6 eggs
145 g (5 oz/^{2}/3 cup) caster (superfine)
  sugar
180 g (6^1/2 oz/1^3/4 cups) ground
  almonds
1 teaspoon baking powder
125 ml (4 fl oz/^{1}/2 cup) mandarin juice
55 g (2 oz/^{1}/4 cup) caster (superfine)
  sugar, extra
poppy seeds, to sprinkle

Preheat the oven to 180°C (350°F/ Gas 4). Put the mandarins in a large saucepan and cover them with water, bring to the boil and then simmer for 2 hours. Drain the mandarins, allow them to cool, then break them into segments and take out any seeds.

Put the fruit and skin into a blender or food processor and purée them. Beat the eggs until light and fluffy, then add the sugar and beat for a further minute before folding in the ground almonds, baking powder and mandarin purée. Pour the mixture into 16 greased muffin tins (lined with paper cases if desired) and bake for 20 minutes.

Put the mandarin juice and sugar in a small saucepan, bring to the boil and simmer for 5 minutes or until the amount of liquid has halved. Remove the cakes from the tins, spoon over the mandarin syrup while they are still warm and sprinkle with poppy seeds.

lemon sorbet

225 g (8 oz/1 cup) sugar
5 lemons, juiced
2 lemons, zest finely grated
1 egg white

Put the sugar and 250 ml (9 fl oz/ 1 cup) water into a saucepan over high heat. Stir until the sugar has dissolved, then remove from the heat. Stir in the zest and juice. Allow to cool, then transfer to a container, cover and refrigerate for 1 hour.

Churn the chilled liquid in an ice cream machine according to the manufacturer's instructions. Whisk the egg white in a bowl until light and frothy. After 30 minutes of churning, add the egg white to the sorbet mixture in the ice cream machine and continue to churn until the sorbet is firm. Serve immediately or store in a covered container in the freezer.

almond macaroons with passionfruit

2 large eggs, separated (discard the yolks)
230 g (8^1/$_2$ oz/1 cup) caster (superfine) sugar
230 g (8^1/$_2$ oz/2^1/$_4$ cups) ground almonds
1 teaspoon natural vanilla extract
icing (confectioners') sugar, to dust
crème fraîche, to serve
fresh passionfruit pulp, to serve

Preheat the oven to 180°C (350°F/ Gas 4). Whisk the egg whites and sugar for about 5 minutes or until the mixture is light and fluffy, then fold in the ground almonds and vanilla extract.

Drop large spoonfuls of the mixture onto baking trays lined with baking paper and bake for 15 minutes or until the macaroons are pale brown. Allow to cool before removing them from the baking tray.

Serve dusted with icing sugar and topped with crème fraîche and some fresh passionfruit.

bread and butter pudding

serves 6

450 g (1 lb) loaf of brioche
1 teaspoon ground cinnamon
3 eggs
3 tablespoons caster (superfine) sugar
500 ml (17 fl oz/2 cups) cream
  (whipping)
4 tablespoons golden (dark corn) syrup
fresh berries, to serve

Preheat the oven to 180°C (350°F/ Gas 4). Lightly butter a ceramic baking dish. Remove the crusts from the brioche, slice the brioche, then cut the slices into triangles. Arrange the triangles over the base of the baking dish and sprinkle with the cinnamon. Put the eggs, caster sugar and cream into a bowl and whisk together. Pour the cream mixture over the brioche and drizzle the golden syrup over the pudding. Bake for 25 minutes, or until the pudding is set and nicely golden brown. Serve with fresh berries.

sago puddings

50 g (1 3/4 oz/1/4 cup) sago
55 g (2 oz/1/4 cup) caster (superfine)
  sugar
500 ml (17 fl oz/2 cups) milk
1 sheet gelatine
40 g (1 1/2 oz/1/3 cup) toasted and finely
  chopped hazelnuts
1/4 teaspoon grated nutmeg
2 tablespoons bitter orange marmalade
150 ml (5 fl oz) cream (whipping),
  whipped
fresh berries or poached fruit, to serve

Put the sago, sugar and milk in a saucepan and bring to the boil. Reduce the heat and simmer for 20 minutes, or until the sago is soft and cooked. Remove from the heat and cool slightly. Soak the gelatine in cold water until soft, squeeze off any excess water and add the gelatine to the warm sago mix. Allow to cool completely. When the sago mix has cooled, fold through the hazelnuts, nutmeg and marmalade. Stir to combine all the ingredients, then fold in the whipped cream. Spoon into 10 small glasses and chill. To serve, top with fresh berries or poached fruit.

mango and orange hearts

serves 6

1 mango
1/2 lemon, juiced
6 sheets gelatine
110 g (3 3/4 oz/1/2 cup) sugar
375 ml (13 fl oz/1 1/2 cups) freshly
  squeezed orange juice
cream (whipping), to serve
lime wedges, to serve

Purée the flesh of the mango with the lemon juice. Pour it into a measuring jug, ensuring that there is 250 ml (9 fl oz/1 cup) of liquid. If it is a little under, top it up with water or orange juice. Set the purée aside.

Fill a large bowl with cold water and soak the gelatine sheets. Meanwhile, put the sugar and orange juice into a small saucepan. Heat, stirring, until the sugar has dissolved, remove the saucepan from the heat and pour the juice into a bowl. Squeeze the water from the gelatine before adding the gelatine to the warm juice. Stir to dissolve and then add the puréed mango. Ladle the liquid into six small 100 ml (3 1/2 fl oz) heart-shaped moulds or ramekins and put them in the fridge for a few hours.

To remove the jellies from the moulds, dip the base of the moulds in warm water and then turn the jellies out onto a plate. Serve with pouring cream and a squeeze of fresh lime juice.

shortbread

185 g (6^{1}/$_{2}$ oz/1^{1}/$_{2}$ cups) plain
 (all-purpose) flour
130 g (4^{3}/$_{4}$ oz/^{3}/$_{4}$ cup) rice flour
200 g (7 oz) unsalted butter, softened
80 g (2^{3}/$_{4}$ oz/^{1}/$_{3}$ cup) caster (superfine)
 sugar
2 teaspoons finely chopped lemon zest
2 tablespoons caster (superfine) sugar,
 extra, to sprinkle

Preheat the oven to 190°C (375°F/ Gas 5). Grease a 30 x 20 cm (12 x 8 in) baking tray and line it with baking paper. Sift the flours, together with a pinch of salt, into a bowl.

Cream the butter and sugar until light and fluffy, and fold through the flours until just combined. Press the mixture into the prepared baking tray and prick all over with a fork. Use a sharp knife to mark 3 cm (1^{1}/$_{4}$ in) squares. Bake for 5 minutes, then reduce the oven temperature to 160°C (315°F/ Gas 2–3) and cook for a further 15– 20 minutes until the shortbread is a pale golden colour.

Sprinkle the lemon zest over the top of the shortbread and cook for a further 5 minutes. Remove from the oven and sprinkle with caster sugar while still warm. Cut into squares and cool on a wire rack.

lemon and coconut tart

serves 8

125 g (4¹/₂ oz) unsalted butter
345 g (12 oz/1¹/₂ cups) caster
  (superfine) sugar
4 large eggs
170 g (5³/₄ oz/1¹/₄ cups) plain yoghurt
1 teaspoon natural vanilla extract
3 tablespoons lemon juice
2 tablespoons lemon zest
90 g (3¹/₄ oz/1 cup) desiccated coconut
1 pre-baked 25 cm (10 in) shortcrust
  tart case (basics)
icing (confectioners') sugar, to dust
cream (whipping) or vanilla ice cream
  (see page 282), to serve

Preheat the oven to 180°C (350°F/ Gas 4). Beat the butter and sugar together until they are light and creamy. Add the eggs one at a time and beat them into the mixture before adding the yoghurt, vanilla, lemon juice and lemon zest. Stir in the coconut and pour the mixture into the pre-baked tart case.

Bake for 30 minutes or until the filling is golden and puffed. Dust with icing sugar and serve warm with cream or ice cream.

schnapps jellies   makes 25 squares

220 g (7³/₄ oz/1 cup) sugar
1 cinnamon stick
2 star anise
4 strips lemon zest
500 ml (17 fl oz/2 cups) apple
   schnapps
12 sheets gelatine
3 sheets edible silver leaf

Put 500 ml (17 fl oz/2 cups) of water in a small saucepan with the sugar, cinnamon, star anise and lemon zest. Bring to the boil, stirring to dissolve the sugar. Reduce the heat and allow the syrup to simmer for 10 minutes. Cool slightly, strain the syrup into a bowl and add the schnapps.

Put the gelatine sheets into a bowl of cold water and leave them to soften for 5 minutes. Squeeze the gelatine of any excess water and add it to the bowl of warm schnapps. Stir until the gelatine has dissolved, then pour the liquid into a 20 x 30 cm (8 x 12 in) baking tray lined with plastic wrap. Lay the sheets of silver leaf over the surface of the jelly. Chill for several hours or overnight, and cut into squares to serve.

orange poppy seed cake

serves 10

250 g (9 oz) softened unsalted butter

225 g (8 oz/1 cup) caster (superfine) sugar

3 lightly beaten eggs

2 tablespoons poppy seeds

1 tablespoon grated orange zest

125 ml (4 fl oz/1/2 cup) milk

250 g (9 oz/2 cups) self-raising flour, sifted

orange icing (basics)

Preheat the oven to 180°C (350°F/ Gas 4). Grease and line a 23 cm (9 in) spring-form cake tin. Beat the butter and sugar in a large mixing bowl. Add the eggs, poppy seeds, orange zest and milk. Stir to combine and then fold in the self-raising flour. Spoon the batter into the prepared cake tin and bake for 1 hour, or until a skewer inserted into the centre of the cake comes out clean. Turn out the cake onto a wire rack to cool. When the cake has cooled, transfer it to a plate and spread with orange icing.

ice cream with wafers makes 5

30 g (1 oz/1/3 cup) desiccated coconut
80 g (23/4 oz/1/4 cup) caster (superfine)
  sugar
1 teaspoon plain (all-purpose) flour
1/4 teaspoon baking powder
40 g (11/2 oz) unsalted butter, melted
1 egg white
500 ml (17 fl oz/2 cups) vanilla ice
  cream (see page 282), to serve

Preheat the oven to 160°C (315°F/ Gas 2–3). Combine the coconut, sugar, flour and baking powder in a bowl. Stir in the melted butter, then add the egg white and whisk until smooth.

Line a baking tray with baking paper and spread a tablespoon of the batter thinly over the baking paper in the tray. Bake for 7 minutes, or until pale gold. Cool slightly, then cut into squares. Repeat until all the wafers have been cooked. Sandwich a slice of ice cream between two wafers and serve.

sticky pineapple cake serves 8

345 g (12 oz/1¹/2 cups) caster
(superfine) sugar
180 g (6¹/2 oz/2 cups) desiccated
coconut, lightly toasted
250 ml (9 fl oz/1 cup) coconut milk
280 g (10 oz/1³/4 cups) diced fresh
pineapple
4 eggs
250 g (9 oz/2 cups) plain (all-purpose)
flour
2 teaspoons baking powder

lime icing
20 g (³/4 oz) unsalted butter, softened
125 g (4¹/2 oz/1 cup) icing
(confectioners') sugar, sifted
2 tablespoons fresh lime juice

Preheat the oven to 180°C (350°F/ Gas 4). Grease and line a round 24 cm (9¹/2 in) spring-form cake tin. Put the sugar, coconut, coconut milk, pineapple and eggs into a large bowl and stir them together. Sift in the flour and baking powder and fold the ingredients together. Spoon the batter into the cake tin and bake for 1 hour.

To make the lime icing, put the butter and icing sugar into a bowl and beat until you have worked the butter into the sugar. Slowly add the lime juice so that the icing is smooth and runny enough to be drizzled.

Test the cake with a skewer to see if it is cooked. Remove the cake from the tin, cool and then gently drizzle over the lime icing.

papaya with
lemon grass syrup   serves 4

220 g (7³/4 oz/1 cup) sugar
2 lemon grass stems, white part only,
   trimmed and bruised
125 ml (4 fl oz/¹/2 cup) passionfruit pulp
2 small red papayas
vanilla ice cream (page 282), to serve

Put the sugar and lemon grass in a small saucepan with 250 ml (9 fl oz/ 1 cup) of water, bring to the boil, then reduce the heat and allow the mixture to simmer for 10 minutes or until it has reduced by half.

Add the passionfruit pulp and stir it in before taking the pan off the heat and allowing it to cool. This syrup will keep for several days in a sealed jar in the fridge. For added flavour, keep the lemon grass in the syrup until you are ready to use it. Gently pour the syrup over the sliced papaya and serve with vanilla ice cream.

eccles cakes

30 g (1 oz/¹/₃ cup) dried peaches,
  chopped
30 g (1 oz/¹/₄ cup) currants
¹/₄ teaspoon ground nutmeg
¹/₄ teaspoon ground allspice
¹/₄ teaspoon ground cinnamon
1 teaspoon caster (superfine) sugar
2 tablespoons orange juice
1 teaspoon finely chopped orange zest
2 teaspoons finely chopped lemon zest
2 sheets ready-made puff pastry,
  thawed
milk, to glaze
icing (confectioners') sugar, to dust

Preheat the oven to 180ºC (350ºF/ Gas 4). Put all the ingredients except the pastry and milk in a bowl and mix well. Stamp out ten rounds of pastry using an 8 cm (3 inch) cookie cutter. Put 1 teaspoon of the fruit mix to one side of each pastry round and fold over to form a half moon. Press the edges together with a fork or your fingers. With a sharp knife, make slits in the top of each pastry.

Put on a baking tray lined with baking paper and brush the tops with a little milk to glaze. Bake for 12–15 minutes, or until golden brown. Remove and lightly dust with icing sugar.

apple vanilla ice with grapefruit

serves 4

4 tablespoons sugar
1 vanilla bean, halved lengthways
1 green apple, grated
200 ml (7 fl oz) cloudy apple juice
2 ruby grapefruits, segmented, to serve

Put 170 ml (5$^1/_2$ fl oz/$^2/_3$ cup) water, the sugar and vanilla into a saucepan and bring to the boil. Stir until the sugar has dissolved, then reduce the heat and stir in the grated apple. Remove from the heat and allow to cool.

Add the apple juice, stir, and put the mixture into a plastic container. Put in the freezer for 1 hour. Remove and stir the mixture with a fork to break up the ice crystals. Return to the freezer for another 1–2 hours. Before serving, stir again with a fork. Serve with the grapefruit segments.

poached pears

350 g (12 oz/1¹/₂ cups) caster
  (superfine) sugar
1 vanilla bean, halved lengthways
2 strips of lemon zest
4 pears

Put the sugar into a heavy-based saucepan with 1 litre (35 fl oz/4 cups) water, the vanilla and lemon zest. Bring to the boil over high heat, stirring until the sugar has dissolved. Remove from the heat.

Peel the pears, leaving the stems on. With the point of a small sharp knife, remove the core from the base of each pear in one circular movement.

Cut a piece of baking paper slightly larger than the size of the saucepan and crumple it up. Stand the pears upright in the syrup and cover with the baking paper. Feel for where the stems are and cut the paper with small scissors so that the stems can stick through. Press the paper down. Cover the saucepan with a lid, put over low heat and gently simmer for 1¹/₂ hours. Remove the saucepan from the heat and allow the pears to cool in the syrup.

caramel slice

125 g (4¹/2 oz/1 cup) plain (all-purpose) flour
90 g (3¹/4 oz) unsalted butter
3 tablespoons caster (superfine) sugar

caramel
400 g (14 oz/1¹/4 cups) condensed milk
30 g (1 oz) unsalted butter
2 tablespoons golden (dark corn) syrup

chocolate
150 g (5¹/2 oz/1 cup) chopped dark eating chocolate

Preheat the oven to 180°C (350°F/ Gas 4). Grease and line a 16 x 26 cm (6¹/4 x 10¹/2 in) slice tin. Put the plain flour, butter and sugar into a food processor and process until it comes together. Remove and press the dough into the base of the tin. Prick the dough with a fork and bake for 15–18 minutes, or until lightly golden.

To make the caramel, put the condensed milk, butter and golden syrup into a saucepan over low heat and stir for 10 minutes. Do not boil. Remove from the heat and set aside to cool for 10 minutes. Pour the caramel over the baked base and return to the oven for 10 minutes, or until the edges of the caramel begin to brown. Remove from the oven and allow to cool and set in the tin.

In a small saucepan, melt the dark eating chocolate and spread it over the cooled caramel. Cut into pieces.

pear and jasmine tea sorbet

serves 4

60 ml (2 fl oz/1/4 cup) lemon juice
4 ya or nashi pears
375 ml (13 fl oz/1 1/2 cups) jasmine tea
80 g (2 3/4 oz/1/3 cup) caster (superfine)
  sugar
fresh lychees, peeled, to serve

Put the lemon juice into a bowl. Peel, core and chop the pears, adding them to the lemon juice as you go. This will prevent them from discolouring. Put the pears and 2 tablespoons of the lemon juice into a saucepan with the tea and sugar and heat over a medium heat. Allow to simmer for 15 minutes or until the pears have become opaque and soft. Blend to a fine purée then pour through a fine sieve into a container. Allow to cool, then cover and put in the freezer for 3 hours or overnight. Remove and scoop into a food processor. Process, then freeze again. Serve scooped into bowls with fresh lychees.

summer punch almond sherbet pear and honey smoothie rockmelon and ginger whip egg flip tamarind and peach cooler lemon cheesecake drink pimm's classic summer morning mango strawberry and apricot chiller citron pressé pina colada fruit daiquiri lychee and champagne chillers banana cardamom lassi banana and honey smoothie mango lassi gin fizz kiwi and citrus cooler punch almond sherbet pear and honey

05   drinks

smoothie rockmelon and ginger whip egg flip tamarind and peach cooler lemon cheesecake drink pimm's classic summer morning mango, strawberry and apricot chiller citron pressé pina colada fruit daiquiri lychee and champagne chillers banana cardamom lassi

summer punch

ginger syrup
1/2 cup grated ginger
220 g (73/4 oz/1 cup) sugar

500 ml (17 fl oz/2 cups) peach nectar
200 ml (7 fl oz) dark rum
60 ml (2 fl oz/1/4 cup) lime juice
3 white peaches, peeled, stones
   removed and finely sliced
160 g (53/4 oz/1 cup) chopped fresh
   pineapple pieces
1 litre (32 fl oz/4 cups) ginger beer or
   ginger wine
fresh lime and mint, to garnish

To make the ginger syrup, put the ginger, sugar and 125 ml (4 fl oz/ 1/2 cup) of water in a small saucepan and bring to the boil. Reduce the heat and simmer for 5 minutes. Strain into a container, cool and store in the refrigerator until ready to use.

To make the punch, put 75 ml (21/2 fl oz/1/3 cup) ginger syrup and the remaining ingredients except the garnishes into a large serving or punch bowl and stir well. Garnish with thinly sliced lime and torn mint leaves.

almond sherbet

4 tablespoons ground almonds
220 g (7³/₄ oz/1 cup) sugar
4 split cardamom pods
1 teaspoon rosewater
2 drops of natural almond extract
2 litres (70 fl oz/8 cups) sparkling water

Put 200 ml (7 fl oz) water, ground almonds, sugar and cardamom pods in a saucepan. Boil until the mixture thickens. Cool, add rosewater and almond extract. Top up with cold sparkling water.

pear and honey smoothie

2 green-skinned pears
1 tablespoon honey
125 g (4¹/₂ oz/¹/₂ cup) plain yoghurt
8 ice cubes

Put all the ingredients in a blender with 125 ml (4 fl oz/¹/₂ cup) of water and blend until smooth. Pour into glasses to serve.

rockmelon and ginger whip

1 tablespoon chopped fresh ginger
330 g (11³/4 oz/2 cups) chopped
   rockmelon (cantaloupe)
125 ml (4 fl oz/¹/2 cup) orange juice
8 ice cubes

Put all the ingredients in a blender and blend until smooth. Pour into tall glasses to serve.

egg flip

250 ml (9 fl oz/1 cup) milk
1 tablespoon plain yoghurt
1 egg
1 tablespoon of honey

Put milk, yoghurt, egg and honey into a blender. Blend until the honey has dissolved, then pour into a chilled glass. Drink immediately.

tamarind and peach cooler

serves 2

2 tablespoons tamarind concentrate
2 ripe peaches, peeled, halved and
   stoned
8 ice cubes

Stir the tamarind concentrate into 250 ml (9 fl oz/1 cup) water. Put the tamarind water, peaches and ice cubes in a blender and blend until smooth. Taste and add a little sugar if desired. Pour into tall glasses.

lemon cheesecake drink

serves 2

125 g (4¹/₂ oz/¹/₂ cup) plain yoghurt
60 ml (2 fl oz/¹/₄ cup) cream (whipping)
2 tablespoons of caster (superfine)
  sugar
2 tablespoons lemon juice
¹/₂ teaspoon natural vanilla extract
6 ice cubes
grated nutmeg, to serve

Blend the yoghurt, cream, sugar, lemon juice, vanilla extract and ice cubes. Pour into glasses and top with grated nutmeg.

pimm's classic

60 ml (2 fl oz/1/4 cup) Pimm's
150 ml (5 fl oz) dry ginger ale
1 teaspoon lime juice
thin slices of orange, to garnish
cucumber strips, to garnish

Put Pimm's, dry ginger ale and lime juice into a tall, chilled glass and top with ice. Stir to combine, then garnish with thin slices of orange and strips of cucumber.

summer morning   serves 2

1/2 **banana**
160 g (5³/4 oz/1 cup) chopped fresh
   pineapple
2 passionfruit, pulped
6 large mint leaves
8 ice cubes

In a blender, combine banana, pineapple, passionfruit pulp, mint leaves and ice cubes. Blend to a smooth consistency and serve immediately in chilled glasses.

mango, strawberry and apricot chiller

serves 2

1 mango
250 ml (9 fl oz/1 cup) apricot nectar
6 strawberries
6 ice cubes

Peel the mango. Put the mango flesh and remaining ingredients in a blender and blend until smooth. Pour into tall glasses to serve.

citron pressé

sugar syrup
220 g (7³/₄ oz/1 cup) sugar

**60 ml (2 fl oz/¹/₄ cup) Absolut citron
  vodka**
2 tablespoons lemon juice
ice, to serve
lemon zest and peel, to garnish

To make sugar syrup, put sugar in a
small saucepan with 250 ml (9 fl oz/
1 cup) of water and bring to the boil,
stirring until the sugar dissolves. Cool,
then store in a bottle in the refrigerator
until ready to use.

Put vodka, 60 ml (2 fl oz/¹/₄ cup) sugar
syrup and lemon juice in a cocktail
shaker. Shake well and pour into a
highball glass containing some ice.
Garnish generously with lemon zest
and a twist of peel.

pina colada

sugar syrup
220 g (7³/4 oz/1 cup) sugar

80 g (2³/4 oz/¹/2 cup) fresh pineapple pieces
6 ice cubes
2 tablespoons lime juice
60 ml (2 fl oz/¹/4 cup) white rum
60 ml (2 fl oz/¹/4 cup) coconut cream
fresh pineapple and lime, to garnish

To make sugar syrup, put sugar in a small saucepan with 250 ml (9 fl oz/ 1 cup) of water and bring to the boil, stirring until the sugar dissolves. Cool, then store in a bottle in the refrigerator until ready to use.

Put 60 ml (2 fl oz/¹/4 cup) sugar syrup and the remaining ingredients except the garnishes in a blender and blend until smooth. Pour into cocktail glasses and decorate with pineapple wedges and thinly sliced lime.

fruit daiquiri serves 2

30 ml (1 fl oz) lime juice
2 teaspoons sugar
2 teaspoons Triple Sec or Cointreau
125 ml (4 fl oz/1/2 cup) white rum
95 g (31/4 oz/1/2 cup) diced mango
80 g (23/4 oz/1/2 cup) diced honeydew
6 ice cubes

In a blender, put lime juice, sugar, Triple Sec or Cointreau, white rum, mango, honeydew and ice cubes. Blend and pour into two chilled glasses.

lychee and champagne
chillers

400 g (14 oz) tin lychees
1 lime, juiced
champagne, to serve

Put the lychees and their syrup into a blender with the lime juice. Blend until smooth and then strain into a jug. Cover and put in the refrigerator for at least 1 hour to chill. Pour the lychee syrup into eight champagne or cocktail glasses and slowly top up each glass with champagne.

banana cardamom lassi serves 2

1 cardamom pod
1 banana, roughly chopped
125 g (4 1/2 oz/1/2 cup) plain yoghurt
9 ice cubes

Remove the small seeds from cardamom pod and put them in a blender along with banana, yoghurt and ice cubes. Blend until smooth. Serve in chilled glasses.

banana and honey smoothie

1 banana, roughly chopped
185 g (6¹/2 oz/³/4 cup) plain yoghurt
1 tablespoon of honey
pinch of nutmeg
8 ice cubes

In a blender, combine the banana, yoghurt, honey, nutmeg and ice cubes. Blend until smooth and serve in glasses immediately.

mango lassi

serves 2

140 g (5 oz/3/4 cup) roughly chopped
  mango flesh
1 teaspoon honey
1 teaspoon lime juice
125 g (41/2 oz/1/2 cup) plain yoghurt
9 cups ice cubes

In a blender, combine mango flesh, honey, lime juice, yoghurt and ice cubes. Blend until smooth and pour into chilled glasses.

gin fizz   serves 1

60 ml (2 fl oz/¹/4 cup) gin
1 tablespoon lemon juice
1 teaspoon caster (superfine) sugar
1 egg white
ice, to fill cocktail shaker
soda water, to serve

Put gin, lemon juice, sugar and a dash of egg white into a cocktail shaker filled with ice. Shake vigorously and pour into a chilled glass. Top with soda water.

kiwi and citrus cooler

serves 4

sugar syrup
220 g (7³/4 oz/1 cup) sugar

1 lime
1 lemon
1 orange
500 ml (17 fl oz/2 cups) orange juice
4 peeled kiwi fruit
60 ml (2 fl oz/¹/4 cup) lime juice

To make the sugar syrup, put sugar in a small saucepan with 250 ml (9 fl oz/ 1 cup) of water and bring to the boil, stirring until the sugar dissolves. Cool, then store in a bottle in the refrigerator until ready to use.

Segment lime, lemon and orange and freeze in ice-cube moulds filled with water. Blend the orange juice, kiwi fruit, lime juice and 2 tablespoons sugar syrup. Pour into glasses over the citrus cubes.

brioche dough harissa chicken stock lemon dipping sauce lemon mayonnaise dashi stock fish stock vegetable stock home-made pizza dough shortcrust pastry lemon and cointreau syrup plum sauce lemon icing orange icing pistachio biscotti mandarin salad vanilla-glazed oranges toffee apples brioche dough harissa chicken stock lemon dipping sauce lemon mayonnaise dashi stock fish stock vegetable

06 basics

stock home-made pizza dough shortcrust pastry lemon and cointreau syrup plum sauce lemon icing orange icing pistachio biscotti mandarin salad vanilla-glazed oranges toffee apples brioche dough harissa chicken stock lemon dipping sauce lemon mayonnaise

brioche dough

50 ml (1 3/4 fl oz) milk
2 teaspoons dry yeast
250 g (9 oz/2 cups) plain (all-purpose)
   flour
35 g (1 1/4 oz) caster (superfine) sugar
3 eggs
1 teaspoon sea salt
125 g (4 1/2 oz) unsalted butter,
   softened

Heat the milk in a small saucepan until it is lukewarm. Remove from the heat and pour into the bowl of an electric mixer. Add the yeast and 3 tablespoons of the flour.

Leave covered for 10 minutes to activate the yeast. When the yeast mix is bubbling on the surface, add the remaining flour, sugar, eggs and sea salt, and begin to mix the dough on a low speed. After a few minutes the dough should start to come together. Add the butter slowly and beat on a higher speed until the dough is shiny and elastic. Transfer to a bowl and cover with plastic wrap. Refrigerate for a minimum of four hours before use.

harissa

2 red capsicums (peppers)
3 red chillies
2 garlic cloves
1 tablespoon cumin seeds, roasted
and ground
1 tablespoon coriander seeds, roasted
and ground
1 large handful coriander (cilantro)
leaves
1 tablespoon pomegranate molasses
1 teaspoon sea salt
2¹/2 tablespoons olive oil

Preheat the oven to 210ºC (415ºF/ Gas 6–7). Put the capsicums in a baking tray and bake for 20 minutes, or until the skin is blistered and blackened. Remove and set aside to cool. When cool, remove the skin and seeds from the capsicums and put the flesh in a food processor with the chillies, garlic, ground spices, pomegranate molasses and sea salt. Blend to purée, then add the olive oil and process again.

chicken stock

makes 2 litres (70 fl oz/8 cups)

1 whole fresh chicken
1 onion, sliced
2 celery sticks, sliced
1 leek, white part only, roughly
  chopped
1 bay leaf
2 flat-leaf (Italian) parsley sprigs
6 whole black peppercorns

Fill a large heavy-based saucepan with 3 litres (105 fl oz/12 cups) of cold water. Cut the chicken into several large pieces and put them into the pan. Bring water just to the boil, then reduce the heat to a simmer. Skim any fat from the surface, then add the onion, celery, leek, bay leaf, parsley and peppercorns. Maintain the heat at a low simmer for 2 hours.

Strain the stock into a bowl and allow to cool. Using a large spoon, remove any fat that has risen to the surface. If a more concentrated flavour is required, return the stock to a saucepan and simmer over low heat. If you are not using the stock immediately, cover and refrigerate or freeze it. Stock will keep in the refrigerator for 2–3 days.

lemon dipping sauce serves 4-6

2 lemons, juiced
2 star anise
3 cardamom pods
45 g (1 1/2 oz/1/4 cup) sugar
2 teaspoons light soy sauce

Put all the ingredients in a small saucepan and simmer over medium heat for 5 minutes. Allow to cool before serving.

lemon mayonnaise serves 4

2 egg yolks
1 lemon, zested and juiced
250 ml (9 fl oz/1 cup) oil

Whisk the egg yolks, lemon zest and juice together in a large bowl. Slowly drizzle in the oil while whisking until the mixture thickens, and keep whisking the mixture until it becomes thick and creamy. Season to taste with sea salt. If the mixture is very thick, add a little cold water until you achieve the right consistency.

dashi stock

makes about 2 litres (70 fl oz/8 cups)

30 g (1 oz) dried kombu
20 g (3/4 oz) bonito flakes

Put 2 litres (70 fl oz/8 cups) cold water and the kombu into a large heavy-based saucepan and slowly bring to the boil over medium heat. Regulate the heat so that the water takes around 10 minutes to come to the boil. As it nears boiling point, test the thickest part of the kombu. If it is soft to the touch and your thumbnail passes easily into the surface, remove from the water.

Once the water is boiling, add 125 ml (4 fl oz/1/2 cup) cold water and the bonito flakes. When the stock returns to the boil, remove the pan from the heat and skim the surface of the stock to remove any muddy froth. When the bonito flakes sink to the bottom, strain the stock into a bowl through muslin cloth or a very fine sieve. The finished stock should be clear and free of bonito flakes.

fish stock

makes about 1 litre (35 fl oz/4 cups)

1 kg (2 lb 4 oz) fish bones
1 onion, chopped
1 carrot, chopped
1 fennel bulb, sliced
2 celery sticks, sliced
2 thyme sprigs
2 parsley sprigs
4 black peppercorns

Put the fish bones into a large saucepan with 2 litres (70 fl oz/ 8 cups) water. Bring just to the boil, then reduce the heat and simmer for 20 minutes. Strain the liquid through a fine sieve into another saucepan to remove the bones and then add the onion, carrot, fennel, celery, thyme, parsley and peppercorns. Bring back to the boil, then reduce the heat and simmer for a further 35 minutes. Strain into a bowl and allow to cool.

vegetable stock

makes about 2 litres (70 fl oz/8 cups)

40 g (1 1/2 oz) unsalted butter
2 garlic cloves, crushed
2 onions, roughly chopped
4 leeks, white part only, coarsely chopped
3 carrots, coarsely chopped
3 celery sticks, thickly sliced
1 fennel bulb, coarsely chopped
1 handful flat-leaf (Italian) parsley
2 thyme sprigs
2 black peppercorns

Put the butter, garlic and onions into a large, heavy-based saucepan. Put the pan over medium heat and stir until the onion is soft and transparent. Add the leeks, carrots, celery, fennel, parsley, thyme and peppercorns. Add 4 litres (140 fl oz/16 cups) water and bring to the boil. Reduce the heat and simmer for 2 hours. Allow to cool. Strain into another saucepan, using the back of a large spoon to press the liquid from the vegetables. Bring the stock to the boil, then reduce the heat to a rolling boil until the stock is reduced by half.

home-made pizza dough

makes 1 quantity pizza dough or 2 medium pizza bases, approximately 23 cm (9 inch) in diameter

2 teaspoons dried yeast or 15 g (1/2 oz) fresh yeast
1 teaspoon sugar
250 g (9 oz/2 cups) plain (all-purpose) flour
1 egg
2 1/2 tablespoons milk
1 teaspoon sea salt

Put the yeast into a small bowl with the sugar and 4 tablespoons warm water. Stir lightly to combine. Set aside for 10–15 minutes, or until the mixture starts to froth. Sift the flour into a bowl and make a well in the centre. Add the egg, milk, sea salt and the yeast mixture. Gradually work the ingredients together to form a stiff dough.

Turn the dough out onto a floured surface and knead until smooth and elastic. Oil a large bowl with a little olive oil and put the dough in it. Rub a little oil over the dough before covering it with a damp cloth. Put the bowl in a warm place for 2 hours, or until the dough has doubled in size.

Preheat the oven to 200°C (400°F/ Gas 6). Divide the dough in half and roll it out on a floured surface. Put the dough onto two greased baking trays and add your toppings. Bake for 15 minutes.

shortcrust pastry

makes one 25 cm (10 in) tart case or 24 tartlet cases

200 g (7 oz/1²/₃ cups) plain
(all-purpose) flour
100 g (3¹/₂ oz) chilled unsalted butter,
cut into cubes
1 pinch of salt for savoury pastry, or
1 tablespoon of caster (superfine)
sugar for sweet pastry

Put the flour and butter into a food processor. Add the salt or sugar and process for 1 minute. Add 2 tablespoons of chilled water and process until the mixture comes together. Wrap the dough in plastic wrap and chill for 30 minutes.

Using a rolling pin, roll out the pastry as thinly as possible over a floured surface, working from the centre outwards. Use the pastry to line a 25 cm (10 in) tart tin or two 12-hole mini tart tins. Chill for a further 30 minutes. Preheat the oven to 180°C (350°F/Gas 4). Prick the base of the pastry case(s), line with crumpled baking paper and fill with uncooked rice or baking weights.

Bake the case(s) for 10–15 minutes, or until the pastry looks cooked and dry. Remove from the oven, remove the baking paper and rice or weights and allow the case to cool.

Uncooked tart cases that are not used immediately can be stored in the freezer for several weeks. Put the prepared tart case into a preheated oven direct from the freezer to prevent the pastry from collapsing in on itself.

lemon and cointreau syrup

makes 100 ml (3¹/₂ fl oz)

3 lemons, juiced
60 g (2¹/₄ oz/¹/₄ cup) sugar
1 star anise
2 tablespoons Cointreau

Put the lemon juice, sugar and star anise in a small saucepan. Bring to the boil, then reduce the heat, allowing the mixture to simmer for a few minutes. Remove from the heat and let it cool before adding Cointreau. This syrup will keep for a couple of weeks in the refrigerator.

plum sauce

1 tablespoon Chinese black vinegar
1 tablespoon rice wine
2 tablespoons sugar
1 teaspoon light soy sauce
1 tablespoon vegetable oil
1$1/2$ teaspoons finely chopped garlic
2 teaspoons grated fresh ginger
4 blood plums, stones removed

Put the vinegar into a small jug or bowl with the rice wine, sugar, soy sauce and 125 ml (4 fl oz/$1/2$ cup) water.
Heat the vegetable oil in a small saucepan over medium heat and add the garlic and ginger. Fry for 1 minute and then add the flesh of the plums. Cook until the plums are beginning to disintegrate, then add the liquid ingredients. Reduce the heat and simmer for 15 minutes, then remove from the heat and cool.

lemon or orange icing (frosting)

makes enough for a 23 cm (9 in) cake or 12 cupcakes

125 g (4¹/₂ oz/1 cup) icing
 (confectioners') sugar, sifted
20 g (³/₄ oz) unsalted butter, softened
1 tablespoon lemon or orange juice

Blend the icing sugar, butter and lemon or orange juice in a mixing bowl. Depending on the desired thickness of your icing, add a little more liquid, a few drops at a time.

Using a spatula or knife, spread the icing over the cooled cake. To get a smooth surface, dip the spatula in warm water and use it to smooth over the icing.

pistachio biscotti

125 g (4¹/2 oz/1 cup) plain
(all-purpose) flour
115 g (4 oz/¹/2 cup) caster (superfine)
sugar
1 teaspoon baking powder
150 g (5¹/2 oz/1 cup) pistachio nuts
2 teaspoons grated orange zest
2 eggs, beaten

Preheat the oven to 180°C (350°F/Gas 4). Mix the flour, sugar, baking powder, pistachio nuts and orange zest together in a large bowl. Make a well in the centre and fold in the eggs to make a sticky dough. Turn out onto a clean floured surface. Divide the dough into 2 sections and roll out each portion to form a log approximately 4 cm (1¹/2 in) in length. Put the logs onto a baking tray lined with baking paper, leaving space for each log to spread a little. Bake for 30 minutes. Remove from the oven and allow to cool.

Reduce the oven temperature to 140°C (275°F/Gas 1). With a sharp bread knife, cut each of the loaves into thin slices, about 5 mm (¹/4 in) wide. Lay the biscuits on a baking tray and return them to the oven. Bake for 20 minutes, turning the biscuits once. Remove from the oven and cool on wire racks.

mandarin salad

6 mandarins
$1/2$ teaspoon orange flower water
$1/2$ teaspoon finely chopped mandarin zest

Segment 4 of the mandarins and put the pieces into a bowl. Squeeze the juice from the remaining 2 mandarins over the segments and add the orange flower water. Add the zest and stir together.

vanilla-glazed oranges

serves 4

4 tablespoons caster (superfine) sugar
4 tablespoons orange juice
1 vanilla bean, halved lengthways
4 oranges, segmented

Put the sugar, juice and vanilla bean in a saucepan and heat them gently together until the sugar dissolves. Turn up the heat and allow the mixture to bubble until it begins to turn thick, sticky and toffee-like.

Add the orange segments and stir them gently into the mixture so that they are completely coated in toffee.

toffee apples

4 green apples, peeled, cored and cut
  into eighths
3 tablespoons caster (superfine) sugar
1 teaspoon ground cinnamon

Toss the apple pieces with the sugar, cinnamon and 2 tablespoons of water. Tip them into a heavy-based frying pan over a medium heat and let them caramelize and brown. Turn each of the apple pieces as they begin to caramelize and take them out when they are cooked on both sides.

glossary

Asian dried shrimp

Dried shrimp are available from most Asian grocery stores and can be bought either whole or shredded. They are used as a flavouring agent in many stocks, or as an ingredient in relishes and sambals.

balsamic vinegar

Balsamic vinegar is a dark, fragrant, sweetish aged vinegar made from grape juice. The production of authentic balsamic vinegar is carefully controlled. Bottles of the real thing have 'Aceto Balsamico tradizionale de Modena' written on the label, while commercial varieties simply have 'Aceto Balsamico de Modena'.

basil

The most commonly used basil is the sweet Genoa variety which is much favoured in Italian cooking. Thai or holy basil is used in Thai and Southeast Asian dishes. To get the most out of basil leaves they should always be torn not chopped.

black sesame seeds

Mainly used in Asian cooking, black sesame seeds add colour, crunch and a distinct nuttiness to whatever dish they garnish. They can be found in most Asian grocery stores. Purchase the seeds regularly, as they can become rancid with age.

buttermilk

This low fat dairy product is made from skim milk and milk powder, with a culture similar to yoghurt. It is often used in baking (as a raising agent) and can be found in the refrigerator section of supermarkets. It has a tart taste.

cardamom

A dried seed pod native to India, cardamom is the third most expensive spice (after saffron and vanilla). The inner seeds when crushed give off a sweet, strong aroma. It is used whole or ground and can be found in the spice section of most supermarkets. Cardamom should be used sparingly, as it has quite a strong flavour.

Chinese black vinegar

This rice vinegar is sharper than white rice varieties and is traditionally used in stir-fries, soups and dipping sauces. The Chinese province of Chekiang has the reputation for producing the best black vinegars.

Chinese five-spice

An aromatic mix of ground spices, Chinese five-spice is made up from star anise, black pepper, fennel seeds, cassia and cloves. It can be rubbed into the skin of chicken or duck or used sparingly to add an exotic flavour to pork or beef.

coconut cream

Slightly thicker than coconut milk, coconut cream is available in tins. If you can't get hold of it, use the thick cream off the top of a couple of tins of coconut milk instead. Pour the milk into a jug and leave it to settle — the cream will separate out at the top.

cream

Cream comes with differing fat contents. If it needs to be whipped it must have a fat content higher than 35 per cent. Single and light cream cannot be whipped.

crème fraîche

A naturally soured cream that is lighter than sour cream. It is available at gourmet food stores and some large supermarkets.

curry leaves

Small, green aromatic leaves of a tree native to India and Sri Lanka. They are usually fried and added to the dish or used as a garnish.

daikon

Daikon, or mooli, is a large white radish. Its flavour varies from mild to surprisingly spicy, depending on the season and variety. Daikon contains an enzyme that aids digestion. It can be freshly grated or slow-cooked in broths, and is available from most large supermarkets or Asian grocery stores. Select firm and shiny vegetables with unscarred skins.

edible silver leaf

Silver leaf, or varak, is flavourless, safe to eat and available from Indian grocery stores. Both gold and silver leaf are also available from cake decorating shops. Both are extremely fragile. Remove the leaf from the paper it is attached to at the last minute by simply turning the paper over and applying the leaf to any surface or liquid.

enoki mushrooms

These pale, delicate mushrooms have a long thin stalk and tiny caps. They are very fragile and need only minimal cooking time.

fish sauce

This is a highly flavoured, salty liquid made from fermented fish and widely used in South Asian cuisine to give a salty, savoury flavour. Buy a small bottle and keep it in the fridge.

gelatine sheets

Gelatine sheets are available in varying sizes. Be careful to check the manufacturer's instructions reagrding which ratio of liquid to gelatine sheet to use.

gruyère cheese

A firm cow's milk cheese with a smooth texture and natural rind. It has a nutty flavour and melts easily, making it perfect for tarts and gratins.

kecap manis
This is a thick, sweet-flavoured soy sauce used in Indonesian cooking.

lemon grass
These long, fragrant stems are very popular in Thai cuisine. The tough outer layers should be stripped off first and it can then be used either finely chopped or whole in soups. Lemon grass can be stored for up to 2 weeks.

makrut leaves
Also known as the kaffir lime, the glossy leaves of this Southeast Asian tree impart a wonderful citrusy aroma. Always try to use fresh, rather than dried leaves.

mascarpone cheese
This heavy, Italian-style set cream is used as a base in many sweet and savoury dishes.

mirin
Mirin is a rice wine used in Japanese cooking. It adds sweetness to many sauces and dressings, and is used for marinating and glazing dishes like teriyaki. It is available from Asian grocery stores and most large supermarkets.

miso paste
An important ingredient in Japanese cooking, miso paste is made of fermented soya beans and other flavourings — wheat, rice or barley. It is used as a flavouring and a condiment.

mizuna
These tender, young salad leaves have a pleasant, peppery flavour.

orange flower water
This perfumed distillation of bitter-orange blossoms is mostly used as a flavouring in baked goods and drinks. It is readily available from large supermarkets and delicatessens.

oyster mushrooms
These delicately flavoured mushrooms are commonly a pale greyish brown or white but are also available in pink and yellow colours. Their flavour is sharp when raw, making them more suitable to use in stir-fried dishes.

palm sugar
Palm sugar (jaggery) is obtained from the sap of various palm trees and is sold in hard cakes or cylinders and in plastic jars. If it is very hard it will need to be grated. It can be found in Asian grocery stores or large supermarkets. Substitute dark brown sugar when palm sugar (jaggery) is unavailable.

pancetta
Pancetta is salted belly of pork. It is sold in good delicatessens, especially Italian ones, and some supermarkets. Pancetta is available either rolled and finely sliced or in large pieces ready to be diced or roughly cut. It adds a rich bacon flavour to dishes.

pickled ginger

Pickled ginger is available from most large supermarkets. The thin slivers of young ginger root are pickled in sweet vinegar and turn a distinct salmon-pink colour in the process.

pomegranate molasses

This is a thick syrup made from the reduction of pomegranate juice. It has a bittersweet flavour, which adds a sour bite to many dishes. It is available from Middle Eastern specialty stores. The closest substitute is sweetened tamarind.

prosciutto

Prosciutto is lightly salted, air-dried ham. It is most commonly bought in paper-thin slices, and is available from delicatessens and large supermarkets. Parma ham and San Daniele are both types of prosciutto.

risotto rice

There are three well-known varieties of risotto rice that are widely available today: Arborio, a large plump grain that makes a stickier risotto; vialone nano, a shorter grain that gives a loose consistency but keeps more of a bite in the middle; and carnaroli, similar in size to vialone nano, which makes a risotto with a firm consistency. All are interchangeable, although cooking times may vary by about 5 minutes or so.

saffron threads

These are the orange-red stigmas of a type of crocus. Saffron is expensive and should be bought in small quantities. Use it sparingly as it has a very strong flavour.

sambal oelek

A hot paste made from pounded chillies, salt and vinegar, it is available from Asian grocery stores and most large supermarkets.

shiitake mushrooms

These Asian mushrooms have white gills and a brown cap. Meaty in texture, they keep their shape well when cooked. Dried shiitake are often sold as dried Chinese mushrooms.

sichuan pepper

Made from the dried red berries of the prickly ash tree, which is native to Sichuan in China. The flavour is spicy-hot and leaves a numbing aftertaste, which can linger for some time. Dry-fry and crush the berries for the best flavour. Japanese sancho pepper is a close relative of sichuan pepper and may be used instead.

somen noodles

These thin, wheat-based Japanese noodles are commonly sold dried and in bundles. They are available from Japanese specialty stores, Asian supermarkets and some health food stores.

star anise

This is a pretty, star-shaped dried fruit that contains small, oval brown seeds. Star anise has a flavour similar to that of anise but is more liquorice-like. It is commonly used whole because of its decorative shape.

sumac

Sumac is a peppery, sour spice made from dried and ground sumac berries. The fruit of a shrub found in the northern hemisphere, it is typically used in Middle Eastern cookery. It is available from most large supermarkets.

tamarind

Tamarind is the sour pulp of an Asian fruit. It is most commonly available compressed into cakes or refined as tamarind concentrate in jars. Tamarind concentrate is widely available; the pulp can be found in Asian food shops. To make tamarind water from compressed tamarind, put 100 g (3 1/2 oz) of tamarind into a bowl and cover with 500 ml (17 fl oz/2 cups) of boiling water. Allow to steep for 1 hour, stirring to break up the fibres, then strain. Use the concentrate according to package instructions.

tofu

This white curd is made from soya beans and is a great source of protein. Bland in taste, it takes on the flavour of the other ingredients. Usually sold in blocks, there are several different types of tofu — soft (silken), firm, sheets and deep-fried.

triticale

This grain is a cross between wheat and rye. It is highly nutritious and is often found in mixed breakfast cereals as well as soups and sweet dishes. It can be bought in health food stores.

vanilla bean

This long, slim black bean has a wonderful caramel aroma which synthetic vanillas can never capture. Good quality vanilla beans should be soft and not too dry. Store unused vanilla pods in a full jar of caster (superfine) sugar, which will not only help to keep the vanilla fresh but the aroma of the bean will quickly infuse the sugar, making it ideal for use in desserts and baking.

water chestnuts

The edible tuber of a water plant, the water chestnut is white and crunchy and adds a delicate texture to many Southeast Asian dishes. Fresh water chestnuts can be bought at Chinese food stores, but they are commonly available whole or sliced in tins.

wonton wrappers

These paper-thin sheets of dough are available either fresh or frozen from Asian grocery stores. They may be wrapped around fillings and steamed, deep-fried or used in broths. The wrappers come shaped both as squares and circles and are available in various thicknesses.

index